POPULAR INTELLIGENCE

BY

V. GALL

SCHOFIELD & SIMS LTD.
HUDDERSFIELD

0 7217 0656 8
Net Edition 0 7217 0657 6

New Edition 1989

Printed in England by
Stott Brothers Limited, Halifax, West Yorkshire

FOREWORD

This book provides a series of carefully prepared exercises with useful hints and examples. The exercises provide pupils of Primary level with excellent practice in logic, number skills and verbal reasoning, making an excellent foundation for further study. Experience has also proved them invaluable for pupils embarking on examinations leading to Secondary education.

The child progresses gradually from simple to more complex exercises, thus learning to read instructions quickly, yet carefully, and to grasp the exact meaning of each question. In this way he or she is able to do exactly what is required in the shortest possible time.

CONTENTS

EXERCISE 1

OBEYING ORDERS

1 Draw a square and put a dot in it.

2 Draw a ring and put a cross in it.

3 Make a cross and put a circle round it.

4 If a square is round, draw a circle round a square; if not, draw a square and put a circle inside it.

5 Draw a triangle inside a square.

6 Draw a circle and put a triangle inside it.

7 Draw a triangle and put a letter "P" inside it.

8 Draw a square and write the word "CAT" inside it.

9 Put four crosses in a row and join the first to the last by a line which passes below the other two crosses.

10 Write the first letter of the alphabet.

11 Write the last letter of the alphabet.

12 Write the longest word of this sentence.

13 Write the shortest word of this sentence.

14 Write the word in front of the longest word in this sentence.

15 Write the word after the shortest word in this sentence.

16 Write a number three less than the number of words in this sentence.

17 Write a number seven more than the number of words in this sentence.

18 Write the word CANADA, then cross out all the A's in the word.

19 Write the word BANANA, then cross out the first N in it.

20 Draw a square and put a smaller square inside it.

EXERCISE 2

THE ALPHABET

A B C D E F G H I J K L M N O P Q R S T U V W X Y Z

1 How many letters are there in the alphabet?

2 Write the first letter of the alphabet.

3 Write the last letter of the alphabet.

4 Write the two middle letters of the alphabet.

5 Write the eleventh letter of the alphabet.

6 Write the last two letters of the alphabet.

7 Write the letter which comes before R.

8 Write the letter which comes after P.

9 Which letter comes before X in the alphabet?

10 Write all the letters between T and P, and underline the middle one.

11 Write the letters which come between G and K.

12 Write the letters between F and L.

13 Write the seventh letter of the alphabet.

14 Write the 23rd letter of the alphabet.

15 Write the 10th letter of the alphabet.

16 Write the letters between V and Z.

17 Write the 25th letter of the alphabet.

18 Write the first and last letters of the alphabet.

19 How many letters are there between the 3rd and the 23rd letters of the alphabet?

20 How many are there between K and Q in the alphabet?

A B C D E F G H I J K L M N O P Q R S T U V W X Y Z
Z Y X W V U T S R Q P O N M L K J I H G F E D C B A

21 If the alphabet were written backwards, which would be the 6th letter?

22 If the alphabet were written backwards, which would be the 9th letter?

23 If the alphabet were written backwards, which would be the last letter?

24 If the alphabet were written backwards, which would be the 19th letter?

EXERCISE 3

THE ALPHABET

A B C D E F G H I J K L M N O P Q R S T U V W X Y Z

1 If E comes before H in the alphabet, and T is found before L, write T, but if only one of these is true, write N.

2 If D comes before H and L comes before S in the alphabet, write X, but if only one of these is true write Z.

3 If L and M come together in the alphabet write P, if not write N.

4 If S and W come together in the alphabet write Y, if not write N.

5 Write the letter which occurs most often in the word SUCCESSFUL.

6 Write the letter which occurs the least often in the word BANANA.

7 If every third letter in the alphabet were lost, what would the 8th letter then be?

8 If Q and R come together in the alphabet write B, if not write the letter which comes after Y in the alphabet.

9 If L and O are separated by three letters in the alphabet, write X, if they are not, write the letter midway between R and V.

10 Write B, unless the 5th letter of the alphabet is H, in which case write W.

11 If LIVERPOOL contains 10th letter of the alphabet write X, but write Z if it does not, unless E is the middle letter of the word MET, in which case write Q.

12 If the word BANANAS has more B's than the word BARGES, write X, if not say how many A's there are in both words.

13 Which of these words contains the first letter of the alphabet more times than any of the other words?
MAT, MANUAL, SLACK, BANANA

14 If snow is white, write W, unless grass is green, in which case write the next letter but one before T in the alphabet.

15 If eyes are used for seeing write S, unless legs are used for walking, in which case write the letter which occurs the most often in the word RESERVOIR.

16 Write the letter which comes 8th in this sentence.

17 Write the letter 5th from the end in this sentence.

EXERCISE 4

THE ALPHABET

A B C D E F G H I J K L M N O P Q R S T U V W X Y Z
Z Y X W V U T S R Q P O N M L K J I H G F E D C B A

1 If after the alphabet, the alphabet were written again backwards as above, which letter would have two letters between its two appearances?

2 Which would have six letters between its two appearances?

3 Which would have four letters between its two appearances?

4 Which would have ten letters between its two appearances?

5 Which would have fourteen letters between its two appearances?

A B C D E F G H I J K L M N O P Q R S T U V W X Y Z

6 If the 1st, 3rd, 5th, 7th, 9th, etc. letters of the alphabet were left out, what would be left of the word CATASTROPHE?

7 What would remain of the word AMERICA?

8 What would be left of the word BANANA?

9 What would be left of the word SCHOLARSHIP?

10 What would remain of the word MONKEY?

A B C D E F G H I J K L M N O P Q R S T U V W X Y Z

11 Suppose the alphabet began at L and read backwards, which would be the 5th letter?

12 Which would be the 3rd letter?

13 Which would be the 9th letter?

14 Which would be the 7th letter?

15 Which would be the last letter?

16 Which would be the 4th letter?

EXERCISE 5

THE ALPHABET

A B C D E F G H I J K L M N O P Q R S T U V W X Y Z
B A D C F E H G J I L K N M P O R Q T S V U X W Z Y

1 Suppose A and B changed places, also C and D and so on. In the alphabet what would the twelfth letter then be?

2 What would the 19th letter be?

3 What would the 7th letter be?

4 What would the 2nd letter be?

5 What would the last letter be?

A B C D E F G H I J K L M N O P Q R S T U V W X Y Z

6 If G and H changed places in the alphabet what would the 8th letter be?

7 If L and K changed places in the alphabet what would the 12th letter be?

A B C D E F G H I J K
K J I H G F E D C B A

8 Suppose the letters A to K were written in the opposite order beginning with K (as above), which letter would remain in the same position?

9 Write the letters which occur the least often in the word COMMITTEE.

10 Write the letter which occurs the most in the word BANANA.

EXERCISE 6

WORDS WRITTEN BACKWARDS

1 T E B A H P L A is a word written backwards. Write it as it should be written.

2 T U A N O R T S A is a word written backwards. Write it as it should be written.

3 T S E B R U O Y O D is made up of three words written backwards. Write them as they should be written.

4 H P A R G O T O H P is a word written backwards. Write it as it should be written.

5 E S N E S N O N is a word written backwards. Write it as it should be written.

6 Write the word C H O C O L A T E backwards.

7 Write the word G E N E R O S I T Y backwards.

8 Write the word B I R T H D A Y backwards.

9 Draw the letters K M F N upside down.

10 Draw the letters P T O X upside down.

11 Which of these words is "spot" spelt backwards:- stop, tops, post?

12 Which of these words is "spin" spelt backwards:- nips, pins, pits?

13 Which of these words is "bats" spelt backwards:- tabs, stab, bast?

14 Which of these words is "star" spelt backwards:- tars, arts, rats?

15 Which of these words is "trap" spelt backwards:- part, rapt, port?

EXERCISE 7

WORDS SEEN IN A MIRROR

Example

Write the word R O C K as it would appear when seen in a mirror. First write the word in capital letters on a card. Hold the card facing a mirror. Look into the mirror and you will see that the card now reads:- ꓘ Ɔ O Я

This shows us two things:-

i The word now appears to be written backwards.

ii The letters all appear to face the wrong way round.

Try several words for yourself and you will see that these results are true every time. When you understand this properly, and can do without your mirror, write the words and letters below as they would appear in a mirror. When you have finished, take out your mirror and see if you are correct.

1 F

2 ERCKS

3 SIT DOWN

4 TRAP

5 BOX

6 MOTOR

7 MACHINE

8 CAMERA

9 BICYCLE

10 CLOCK

The following were seen in a mirror. How should they be written? Remember that the mirror shows words written backwards, also the letters are seen facing the wrong way.

11 ⅃ O O H Ɔ Ƨ

12 O И A I ꟼ

13 Ǝ T I ꓘ

14 ⅃ ⅃ A ᗺ T O O ꟻ

15 Y Ǝ ꓘ И O ᗡ

EXERCISE 8

CODE WRITING

Example 1
If *X P Z O G* means "PLEAD", then *X O P Z* means dale, pale, lead. Which?
Place the code letters exactly above the word which they represent.

X P Z O G We see at once from this that *X*=P, *P*=L, *Z*=E, *O*=A and *G*=D.
P L E A D Therefore *X O P Z* must mean PALE.

Example 2
If *S Z K W X* means TORCH, then *X Z S* means hot, ton, rot. Which?
As before, place the code letters above the word which they represent.

S Z K W X We see that *S*=T, *Z*=O, *K*=R, *W*=C and *X*=H.
T O R C H Therefore *X Z S* must mean HOT.

Now work out the following words in code writing. Set them down exactly as in the examples above.

1 If *K Z W N X* means REACH, then *N W K Z* means ache, hear, care. Which?

2 If *F X Z P W* means SCORE, then *P Z F W* means core, sore, rose. Which?

3 If *W B Z X K S* means CARPET, *X B Z K* means trap, cart, pare. Which?

4 If *X W K Z K Q F* means PRESENT, *Z X K Q F* means spent, trees, steep. Which?

5 *W R B X Q P Z* means KITCHEN, *Q R Z B* means chin, tick, hint. Which?

6 *X Z W P X B Q* means ANIMALS, Therefore *Q X W B* means mail, nail, sail. Which?

7 If *K W Z X Q B* means CANDLE, then *Q W K B* means cane, land, lace. Which?

8 If *Z W X Q B K* means PLACED, then *Q W X Z* means peal, cape, deal, lead, clap. Which?

EXERCISE 9

CODE WRITING

In a piece of secret writing *XPKC WZMBCLPK ZTFP* means:- SEND CHILDREN HOME.

Place the code words exactly above the words of the given message:-
X P K C   W Z M B C L P K   Z T F P
S E N D   C H I L D R E N   H O M E

You will see at once that *X*=S, *P*=E, *K*=N, *C*=D, *W*=C and so on.

Now give the meaning of the following code messges.

1 *FTLP XWZTTBX ZPLP.*

2 *WZMBCLPK CT ZTFP BPXXTKX.*

In a piece of secret writing *KMXPZJRL PXBR DWFRT* means:- CHILDREN LIKE GAMES.

As before place the code letters exactly above the words they represent.
K M X P Z J R L   P X B R   D W F R T
C H I L D R E N   L I K E   G A M E S

You will see at once that *K*=C, *M*=H, *X*=I, *P*= L and so on.

Now give the meaning of the following code messages.

3 *PXLZW XT W LWFR.*

4 *KMWJPRT KWL TXLD.*

EXERCISE 10

CODE WRITING

A	B	C	D	E	F	G	H	I	J	K	L	M	N	O	P	Q	R	S	T	U	V	W	X	Y	Z
1	2	3	4	5	6	7	8	9	10	11	12	13	14	15	16	17	18	19	20	21	22	23	24	25	26

If A=1, B=2, C=3, and so on, we see the word C A B is represented by the numbers 3, 1, 2.

Now write the words represented by the following:-

1 4 9 7

2 2 15 25

3 3 1 11 5

4 3 1 14 25 15 21 16 12 1 25 20 8 5 6 12 21 20 5?

5 9 14 11 9 19 2 12 1 3 11

6 7 15 8 15 13 5 14 15 23

Translate the following message in code by writing underneath the letters for which the figures stand. Use the table at the top of the page.

7 20 1 11 5 20 8 9 19 12 5 20 20 5 18 20 15
20 8 5 16 15 19 20 15 6 6 9 3 5 16 12 5 1 19 5

Put the following into the same code:-

8 Say nothing.

9 Work hard.

10 Stand still.

Translate these numbers into words.

11 5 1 20 25 15 21 18 6 15 15 4

12 4 15 25 15 21 18 2 5 19 20

EXERCISE 11

NUMBER SERIES

Example 1
What is the next number in the following:- 2, 4, 6, 8, 10, 12, *?
Now you will see at once that 2 has been added on every time, so that the missing number must be 12+ 2 which is 14.

In the following exercises a different number has been added in each case. Find these numbers and then write the missing numbers in your exercise book.

1 6, 8, 10, 12, 14, *

2 1, 3, 5, 7, 9, *

3 3, 6, 9, 12, 15, *

4 1, 5, 9, 13, 17, *

5 2, 7,12, 17, 22, *

6 1, 11, 21, 31, 41, *

7 1, 8, 15, 22, 29, *

8 2, 8, 14, 20, 26, *

9 2, 5, 8, 11, 14, *

10 5, 10, 15, 20, 25, *

Example 2
11, 9, 7, 5, 3, *
In the example above you will see that 2 has been taken away every time, so the missing number is 3 – 2 which is 1.

What are the missing numbers in the exercises below?

11 12, 10, 8, 6, 4, *

12 13, 10, 7, 4, *

13 9, 8, 7, 6, 5, *

14 16, 12, 8, 4, *

15 35, 30, 25, 20, *

16 36, 30, 24, 18, 12, *

17 21, 14, 7, *

18 15, 13, 11, 9, *

19 17, 14, 11, *

20 250, 200, 150, *

EXERCISE 12

NUMBER SERIES

Example 1

Find the next number in the following:- 1, 2, 4, 8, 16, *
You will see that each number has been doubled or multiplied by 2.
Therefore the missing number must be the last number multiplied by 2, that is 16X 2 which = 32.

What are the missing numbers in the following exercises, first finding the number by which you must multiply the last number?

1 1, 3, 9, 27, 81, *

2 2, 4, 8, 16, 32, *

3 1, 4, 16, 64, *

4 1, 5, 25, 125, *

5 1, 10, 100, 1000, *

6 1, 6, 36, 216, *

7 2, 6, 18, 54, *

8 3, 6, 12, 24, 48, *

9 2, 10, 50, 250, *

10 3, 9, 27, 81, 243, *

Example 2

What is the missing number in the following:- 81, 27, 9, 3, *?
You will see that this time every number has been divided by 3.
Therefore the missing number must be the last number divided by 3.
We then have 3 divided by 3, which = 1.

Now find the missing numbers in the following. You must first find the number by which you must divide.

11 243, 81, 27, 9, *

12 24, 12, 6, *

13 625, 125, 25, 5, *

14 256, 128, 64, 32, *

15 96, 48, 24, 12, 6, *

16 27, 9, 3, 1, *

17 25, 5, 1, *

18 216, 36, 6, 1, *

19 1000, 100, 10, *

20 27, 9, 3, *

EXERCISE 13

NUMBER SERIES

Example 1
What is the next number in the series? 8, 9, 11, 12, 14, 15, *
The rule here is:- add 1 then add 2, add 1 then add 2, and so on. Thus the next number is 15 plus 2 which = 17.

Before working the following, read carefully and find the rule for each.

1 1, 2, 4, 5, 7, 8, *

2 2, 3, 5, 6, 8, *

3 3, 4, 6, 7, 9, 10, *

4 9, 10, 12, 13, 15, *

5 21, 22, 24, 25, 27, *

Example 2
What is the next number in the following series? 10, 7, 9, 6, 8, 5, *
The rule here is:- take away 3 then add 2, take away 3 then add 2, and so on. Thus the next number is 5 plus 2 which = 7.

Now work out the following:-

6 6, 3, 5, 2, 4, *

7 9, 6, 8, 5, 7, *

8 12, 9, 11, 8, 10, *

9 20, 17, 19, 16, 18, 15, *

10 13, 10, 12, 9, 11, *

In the following, find the rule for yourself, then write the answers in your exercise book. You must find *two numbers* this time.

11 14, 13, 15, 14, 16, * *

12 9, 8, 10, 9, 11, 10, * *

13 3, 2, 4, 3, 5, 4, * *

14 21, 20, 22, 21; 23, * *

15 5, 4, 6, 5, 7, * *

EXERCISE 14

NUMBER SERIES

Example 1
What is the next number in the following? 3, 7, 13, 21, 31, *
The rule here is:- add 4, add 6, add 8, add 10, add 12, and so on.
The missing number is therefore 31 + 12 = 43.

Now work the following exercises. A different number must be added every time. Write your answers in your exercise book.

1 1, 5, 11, 19, *

2 2, 6, 12, 20, 30, *

3 3, 7, 13, *

4 4, 8, 14, 22, *

5 5, 9, 15, *

Example 2
What is the next number in the following? 1, 4, 8, 11, 22, *
The rule here is:- add 3, double the answer, add 3, double the answer, and so on. The missing number is therefore 22 + 3 = 25. The next number in the series would be 25 + 25 = 50.

Now work the following:-

6 2, 5, 10, 13, 26, *

7 3, 6, 12, 15, 30, 33, *

8 0, 3, 6, 9, 18, 21, *

9 1, 4, 8, 11, *

10 5, 8, 16, 19, *

In the following examples find the rule for yourself:-

11 66, 45, 28, 15, 6, *

12 72, 49, 30, 15, *

13 96, 70, 48, *

14 84, 60, 40, 24, *

15 100, 72, 48, 28, *

16 80, 56, 36, 20, *

EXERCISE 15

NUMBER SERIES

Example 1
What is the missing number? 2, 4, 5, 10, 11, 22, *
The rule here is:- double the number, then add 1, double the number you now have, then again add 1, and so on. Thus the missing number is 22 + 1 which makes 23, the next number in this series would be 23 + 23 = 46.

Now work the following exercises. Find out the rule for each before you start. Write your answers in your exercise book

1 3, 6, 7, 14, 15, *

2 2, 4, 5, 10, 11, 22, 23, *

3 4, 8, 9, 18, 19, *

4 1, 2, 3, 6, 7, 14, *

5 5, 10, 11, 22, 23, *

Example 2
What is the missing number in the following? 1, 4, 9, 16, 25, 36, *
The rule here is:- add 3, add 5, add 7, add 9, add 11, and so on. Thus the missing number is 36 + 13 which = 49.

Now work the following:-

6 2, 5, 10, 17, *

7 4, 7, 12, *

8 5, 8, 13, 20, *

9 6, 9, 14, 21, *

10 7, 10, 15, 22, 31, *

In the following find out the rule for yourself:-

11 2, 3, 5, 8, 12, *

12 0, 1, 3, 6, 10, 15, *

13 3, 4, 6, 9, 13, 18, *

14 4, 5, 7, 10, 14, *

15 5, 6, 8, 11, *

EXERCISE 16

NUMBER SERIES

Example 1
Write out and complete the missing number in the following:-
2, 3, 6, 7, 10, 11, * The rule here is:- add 1, add 3, add 1, add 3, and so on. The next number is therefore 11 + 3 which is 14. The next number would be 14 + 1 = 15. Read the examples below very carefully and find the rule for each line.

Then write out and complete the answers.

1 1, 2, 5, 6, 9, 10, 13, *

2 2, 3, 6, 7, 10, 11, 14, *

3 5, 6, 9, 10, 13, 14, *

4 4, 5, 8, 9, 12, *

5 0, 1, 4, 5, 8, *

Example 2
Fill in and complete the missing number in the following:-
9, 12, 10, 13, 11, 14, * Here the rule is:- add 3, take away 2, add 3, take away 2, and so on. The missing number is therefore 14 – 2 which = 12. The next number would be 12 + 3 = 15.

Write out and complete the missing numbers in the following.
Find the rule for each example first.

6 1, 4, 2, 5, 3, 6, *

7 2, 5, 3, 6, 4, *

8 7, 10, 8, 11, 9, 12, *

9 5, 8, 6, 9, 7, *

10 6, 9, 7, 10, 8, *

EXERCISE 17

NUMBER SERIES

Example 1
Fill in the missing number in the following:-

$\frac{1}{2}$ $\frac{1}{4}$ $\frac{1}{6}$ $\frac{1}{8}$ $\frac{1}{10}$ *

The rule here is:- add 2 to the denominator each time.
Thus the new number is $\frac{1}{12}$.

Now work out the following:-

1 $\frac{1}{4}$ $\frac{1}{6}$ $\frac{1}{8}$ $\frac{1}{10}$ $\frac{1}{12}$ *

2 $\frac{1}{3}$ $\frac{1}{5}$ $\frac{1}{7}$ $\frac{1}{9}$ *

3 $\frac{1}{5}$ $\frac{1}{7}$ $\frac{1}{9}$ $\frac{1}{11}$ *

4 $\frac{1}{7}$ $\frac{1}{9}$ $\frac{1}{11}$ $\frac{1}{13}$ *

5 $\frac{1}{4}$ $\frac{1}{6}$ $\frac{1}{8}$ $\frac{1}{10}$ *

6 $\frac{1}{8}$ $\frac{1}{4}$ $\frac{1}{2}$ 1 *

7 $\frac{1}{4}$ $\frac{1}{2}$ $\frac{3}{4}$ 1 *

8 $2\frac{3}{4}$ $2\frac{1}{4}$ $1\frac{3}{4}$ *

9 $4\frac{1}{2}$ 4 $3\frac{1}{2}$ 3 $2\frac{1}{2}$ *

EXERCISE 18

NUMBERS

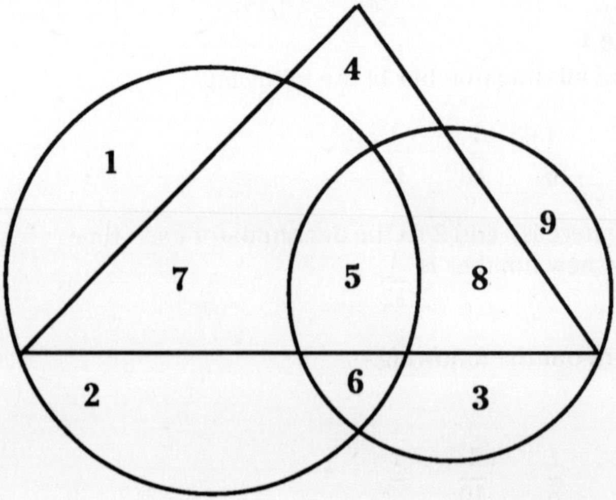

Here you have a triangle and two circles. One circle is larger than the other. Numbers have been placed inside these three figures. If you look carefully you will notice that some of the numbers are in all three of the figures, while some are in two figures, or in one only.

Now answer the following:-

1 Which number is inside both circles but not inside the triangle?

2 Which numbers are inside the small circle only?

3 Which numbers are inside the large circle only?

4 Which number is inside the triangle, but in no other figure?

5 Which number is inside the triangle and small circle only?

6 Which number is inside the triangle and large circle only?

7 Which number is inside all three figures?

8 Add up all the numbers that are inside the triangle.

9 Add up all the numbers which come inside only one figure.

10 Take away the sum of the numbers which come inside the large circle only from the sum of the numbers which come in the small circle only.

EXERCISE 19

NUMBERS

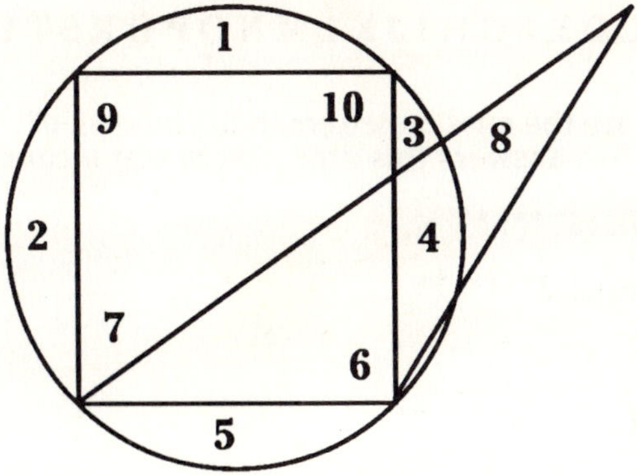

1 Which number is in the triangle only?

2 Which numbers are in the circle only?

3 Which numbers are in the square and circle but not inside the triangle?

4 Which numbers are inside the triangle and the circle but not inside the square?

5 Which number is in all three figures?

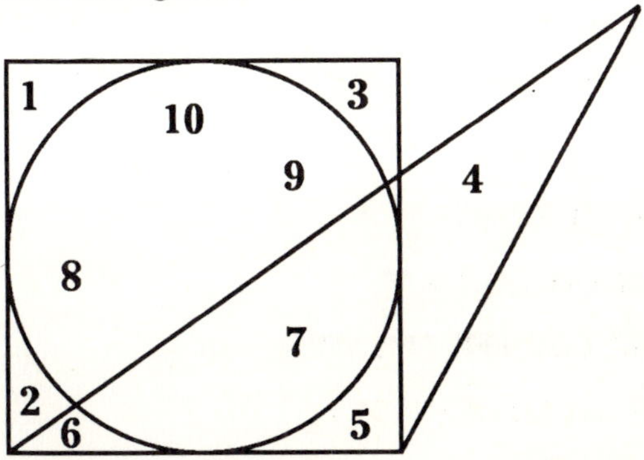

6 Which numbers are inside the square only?

7 Which number is inside the triangle only?

8 Which numbers are inside the circle only?

9 Which number is inside all three figures?

10 Which numbers are inside the square and the triangle but not inside the circle?

EXERCISE 20

LETTER SERIES

A B C D E F G H I J K L M N O P Q R S T U V W X Y Z

What are the missing letters in the following? *Notice* that you will have two answers this time. Every star means a letter.

1 AB, CD, EF, **, **

2 AC, DF, GI, JL, **, **

3 AB, BC, CD, DE, **, **

4 AD, DG, GJ, JM, **, **

5 ABC, DEF, GHI, ***, ***

6 AZ, BY, CX, DW, **, **

7 BB, DD, FF, HH, **, **

8 ACE, HJL, ***, ***

9 OO, QQ, SS, UU, **, **

10 DDD, HHH, LLL, ***, ***

11 DA, HE, LI, **, **

12 BC, EF, HI, **, **

13 AZ, YB, CX, WD, **, **

14 ZA, YB, XC, WD, **, **

15 MM, OO, QQ, SS, **, **

16 ABZ, CDY, EFX, ***, ***

17 AB, DE, GH, JK, **, **

18 LMN, OPQ, RST, ***, ***

19 BA, DC, FE, **, **

20 CBA, FED, IHG, ***, ***

From the following lists, write out the one which is different.

21 AB, EF, LM, ON, UV

22 CD, HI, NO, AC, WX

EXERCISE 21

LETTER SERIES

IF A = 3, B = 2, C = 4, and D = 1 then A + B = 3 + 2 = 5.
Also A + B + C + D = 3 + 2 + 4 + 1 = 10.
Also B + D = 2 + 1 = 3.

Now if A = 1, B = 5, C = 3, and D = 7, find the value of the following:-

1 A + D

2 C + B

3 A + C + D

4 B + C + A

5 Which letters add up to 15?

6 Which letters add up to 11?

7 Which letters add up to 8?

8 Which letters add up to 10?

9 Which letters add up to 6?

10 Which letters add up to 9?

If A = 1, B = 2, C = 3, D = 4, E = 5:-

11 Which letters add up to 12?

12 Which letters add up to 6?

13 Which letters add up to 15?

14 Which letters add up to 10?

15 B + D – A Give your answer as a *letter.*

16 C + B – D Give your answer as a *letter.*

17 A + B + C Give your answer as a *number.*

18 B + D – C Give your answer as a *number.*

19 A + B Give your answer as a *letter.*

20 E + A – D Give your answer as a *letter.*

EXERCISE 22

MISSING NUMBERS

Copy the following into your exercise book and find out the missing numbers

1
```
 3 9 1 6 -
 1 4 * 8
 -------
 2 4 3 8
 =======
```

2
```
 6 * 3 0 4 -
 4 2 9 8 7
 ---------
 2 5 3 1 7
 =========
```

3
```
 7 4 6 3 -
 2 8 5 *
 -------
 4 6 0 4
 =======
```

4
```
 9 1 6 3 7 -
 2 7 4 7 *
 ---------
 6 * 1 5 9
 =========
```

5
```
 9 * 4 7 -
 2 8 7 5
 -------
 6 2 7 2
 =======
```

6
```
 8 6 4 6 3 -
 2 0 9 * 4
 ---------
 6 * 4 8 9
 =========
```

7
```
   2 * 7 X
       5
 -------
 1 1 8 5
 =======
```

8
```
   4 0 * X
       3
 -------
 1 2 2 1
 =======
```

9
```
   5 * 3 X
       7
 -------
 3 9 4 1
 =======
```

10
```
   6 3 * X
       5
 -------
 3 1 7 5
 =======
```

EXERCISE 23

MISSING NUMBERS

What are the missing numbers in the following?

1
$$\begin{array}{r} 6\,7\,1\,3\,6 \; - \\ 2\,8\,4\,*\,9 \\ \hline 3\,8\,7\,1\,7 \\ \hline\hline \end{array}$$

2
$$\begin{array}{r} 2\,*\,7\,1\,3 \; - \\ 1\,5\,8\,7\,6 \\ \hline 1\,2\,8\,3\,7 \\ \hline\hline \end{array}$$

3
$$\begin{array}{r} 9\,6\,0\,2\,7 \; - \\ 4\,3\,8\,7\,* \\ \hline 5\,2\,1\,4\,8 \\ \hline\hline \end{array}$$

4
$$\begin{array}{r} 8\,0\,6\,7\,1 \; - \\ 2\,9\,3\,4\,* \\ \hline 5\,*\,3\,2\,4 \\ \hline\hline \end{array}$$

5
$$\begin{array}{r} 8\,*\,7\,1\,5 \; - \\ 2\,9\,4\,7\,6 \\ \hline 5\,4\,2\,3\,9 \\ \hline\hline \end{array}$$

6
$$\begin{array}{r} 6\,6\,3\,5\,8 \; - \\ 2\,7\,6\,*\,9 \\ \hline 3\,*\,7\,1\,9 \\ \hline\hline \end{array}$$

7
$$\begin{array}{r} 2\,*\,3 \; \times \\ 6 \\ \hline 1\,7\,5\,8 \\ \hline\hline \end{array}$$

8
$$\begin{array}{r} 4\,0\,* \; \times \\ 3 \\ \hline 1\,2\,1\,8 \\ \hline\hline \end{array}$$

9
$$\begin{array}{r} 3\,*\,6 \; \times \\ 5 \\ \hline 1\,5\,8\,0 \\ \hline\hline \end{array}$$

10
$$\begin{array}{r} 4\,7\,* \; \times \\ 9 \\ \hline 4\,2\,5\,7 \\ \hline\hline \end{array}$$

EXERCISE 24

MISSING NUMBERS

What are the missing numbers in the following?

1

```
 6 7 3 1 -
 2 8 * 7
 -------
 3 8 3 4
 =======
```

2

```
 8 6 6 9 -
 2 * 7 3
 -------
 6 1 9 6
 =======
```

3

```
 9 6 1 7 -
 2 8 0 *
 -------
 6 * 0 8
 =======
```

4

```
 8 * 4 6 -
 2 9 7 8
 -------
 5 3 6 8
 =======
```

5

```
 3 * 6 2 5 -
 1 5 9 1 6
 ---------
 2 1 7 0 9
 =========
```

6

```
 3 * 8 4 5 -
 2 5 9 3 6
 ---------
 1 3 9 0 9
 =========
```

7

```
   2 * 3 X
       5
 -------
 1 3 1 5
 =======
```

8

```
   3 * 6 X
       8
 -------
 2 8 4 8
 =======
```

9

```
   4 * 3 X
       6
 -------
 2 7 7 8
 =======
```

10

```
   5 * 2 X
       7
 -------
 3 7 2 4
 =======
```

EXERCISE 25

MISSING WORDS

What are the correct words in the following? Each dot represents a letter.

1 in, inset on, onset off, offset out, ...

2 cast, forecast finger, forefinger father, ...

3 card, postcard script, postscript man, ...

4 friend, befriend little, belittle calm, ...

5 come, outcome lay, outlay side, ...

6 hand, underhand mine, undermine stood, understood fed, ...

7 thought, afterthought noon, afternoon glow, ...

8 cast, overcast shadow, overshadow head, ...

9 stairs, downstairs trodden, downtrodden cast, ...

10 spell, spellbound storm, stormbound weather, ...

11 top, pot spin, nips nap, . . .

12 pat, tap pal, lap dab, . . .

13 spot, tops stab, bats rats, ...

14 three, thirty seven, seventy six, ...

15 two, twenty eight, eighty seven, ...

16 one, first five, fifth three, ...

17 ten, tenth six, sixth two, ...

18 three, thirteen six, sixteen seven, ...

19 part, trap nuts, ...

20 ward, draw evil, ...

21 maid, made pail, ...

22 steel, steal beach, ...

23 piece, peace boy, ...

24 meet, meat great, ...

25 tail, tale wood, ...

26 rough, ruff bough, ...

27 pear, pare waste, ...

28 knead, need pain, ...

29 foul, fowl sow, . . .

30 fore, four sore, ...

EXERCISE 26

WORDS AND NUMBERS IN CORRECT ORDER

Arrange the following lists of words and numbers in correct order. The first is done for you.

1 nail arm hand finger — nail finger hand arm

2 Tuesday Friday Monday Thursday Saturday

3 five pence one pound ten pence two pence

4 May August December March June

5 night dawn morning noon evening

6 fruit shoot seed flower leaf

7 1952 1923 1432 1784

8 2354 4536 8765 4567

9 week month hour minute fortnight

10 gram kilogram milligram

11 centimetre kilometre metre millimetre

12 x v vi iv ix

13 2.7 3.7 4.6 9.1 5.3

14 4 p.m. 2 p.m. 7 a.m. 6 p.m. 3 p.m. 5 a.m.

15 half quarter eighth one

16 2.30 p.m. 6.15 a.m. 1.30 p.m. 2.45 p.m. 4 p.m.

17 breakfast dress school walk wash

18 line chapter word page book.

19 iii v ii viii iv

20 run walk loiter stand

21 kilolitre millilitre litre

22 £1·35 £0·50 £3·67 £1·25

23 flour grain mill bread

24 ten pence fifty pence two pence one pound

EXERCISE 27

SAMES AND OPPOSITES

Learn these words and find their meanings from your dictionary.
TRANSPARENT OPAQUE CONSPICUOUS OBSCURE CONTRACT
EXPAND OPTIMIST PESSIMIST ABRUPT BRIEF

1 What are the missing words in the following? Look at the list above.

a She found the book immediately for it was ______________ on the shelf.
b She did not understand for the meaning was ______________
c He filled the balloon in order to make it ______________
d As the glass was ______________ she could see through it.
e It was a very ______________ note containing only a few sentences.

2 Write words opposite in meaning to the words listed at the top of the page.

3 In the following pairs of words write S if they have the same or nearly the same meaning, and D if their meaning is different.

a transparent ________ clear
b conspicuous _____ hidden
c abrupt __________ sudden
d brief ______________ short
e obscure ____________ clear
f opaque ___________ visible
g expand ___________ enlarge
h contract _________ decrease
i pessimist ________ optimist
j optimist ____________ miser

4 Look at the first word and then at the words in brackets on the same line. From the words in brackets, find a word which means nearly the same or nearly the opposite of the first word. Write out this word, then underline it if it means the same.

a transparent ______________________ (clear, dull, glass)
b conspicuous ______________________ (visible, sudden, bright)
c abrupt ______________________ (sudden, broken, short)
d brief ______________________ (short, alone, bright)
e obscure ______________________ (hidden , bright, lonely)
f opaque ______________________ (transparent, shady, open)
g expand ______________________ (enlarge, heat, change)
h contract ______________________ (break, decrease, take)
i pessimist ______________________ (optimist, hero, knave)
j optimist ______________________ (miser, pessimist, idler)

EXERCISE 28

SAMES AND OPPOSITES

Learn these words and find their meanings from your dictionary.
GRADUALLY MONOTONOUS PERPETUAL MAGNIFY
MINIMUM ENCOURAGE MAXIMUM DISCOURAGE
DECREASE SELDOM

1 What are the missing words in the following? Use the list of words above.

- **a** His movements _______________ became slower and slower.
- **b** Her speech was very _______________ and the children ceased to listen.
- **c** _______________ means going on forever.
- **d** He looked through a lens in order to _______________ the object.
- **e** He had done very little work so he received the _______________ wage.

2 Look at the following pairs of words. Write S if they have the same or nearly the same meaning, and D if their meaning is different.

- **a** MAXIMUM _______ utmost
- **b** DISCOURAGE_________ help
- **c** PERPETUAL _____ ceaseless
- **d** MAGNIFY__________ enlarge
- **e** DECREASE__________ lessen
- **f** SELDOM ___________ frequently
- **g** MONOTONOUS____ interesting
- **h** GRADUALLY_________ quickly
- **i** MINIMUM ______________ least
- **j** VISIBLE _______________unseen

3 Look at the first word and then at the words in the brackets on the same line. From the words in brackets, find a word which means nearly the same or nearly the opposite of the first word. Write it and underline it if it means the same.

- **a** MAGNIFY ______________________ (belittle, prize, together, strength)
- **b** DISCOURAGE ___________________ (no, deter, help)
- **c** ENCOURAGE ____________________ (urge, respond, hope)
- **d** BELITTLE ______________________ (small, magnify, despise)
- **e** GRADUALLY ____________________ (now, slowly, immediately)
- **f** MAXIMUM ______________________ (grand, highest, present)

EXERCISE 29

SAMES AND OPPOSITES

Learn these words and find their meanings from your dictionary.
INFERIOR RARELY FATIGUED SUPERIOR FREQUENTLY
PROSPEROUS IMPERTINENT ABANDON POLITE NONSENSE

1 What are the missing words in the following? They are all in the list above.

a She was __________ as she had walked a long way.
b He __________ read the newspaper for he had very poor eyesight.
c He loitered on his way to school so he was __________ late.
d Her work was __________ to that of any other child, so she was rewarded.
e A good mother will never __________ her child.

2 Look at the following pairs of words. Write S if they have the same or nearly the same meaning, and D if their meaning is different.

a FATIGUED __________________ healthy
b SELDOM __________________ often
c FREQUENTLY __________________ never
d POLITE __________________ rude
e IMPERTINENT __________________ bad-mannered
f RARELY __________________ seldom
g INFERIOR __________________ worse
h SUPERIOR __________________ better
i NONSENSE __________________ sense
j ABANDON __________________ take

3 Look at the first word and then at the words in brackets on the same line. From the words in the brackets, find a word which means nearly the same or nearly the opposite of the first word. Underline it in your exercise book if it means the same.

a FATIGUED __________________ (bright, sunny, exhausted)
b RARELY __________________ (often, sometimes, seldom)
c FREQUENTLY __________________ (again, now, seldom)
d SUPERIOR __________________ (better, less, more, again)
e INFERIOR __________________ (worse, good, best, never)
f NONSENSE __________________ (rhyme, foolishness, talk)
g ABANDON __________________ (take, receive, leave)

EXERCISE 30

SAMES AND OPPOSITES

Learn these words and find their meanings from your dictionary.
DUBIOUS CERTAIN INDOLENT ENERGETIC NIMBLE
CLUMSY FLIMSY IGNORANT MODERATION EXCESS

1 What are the missing words in the following? Use the words above.

a He was __________ and did as little work as possible.
b The __________ woman kept her house very clean and tidy.
c She was very quick and __________ in her movements.
d A __________ person often drops things.
e The dress was easily torn for it was made of very __________ material.

2 Write words opposite in meaning to the words at the top of the page.

3 In the following list of words write S if they have the same or nearly the same meaning, and D if their meaning is different.

a INDOLENT __________________ lazy
b ENERGETIC __________________ active
c NIMBLE __________________ clumsy
d CLUMSY __________________ awkward
e DUBIOUS __________________ certain
f CERTAIN __________________ sure
g IGNORANT __________________ learned
h MODERATION __________________ excess

4 From the words in the brackets find a word which means nearly the same or nearly the opposite of the first word. Underline it in your exercise book if it means the same. Write O after it if it means the opposite.

a INDOLENT __________________ (happy, lazy, careful, pleasant)
b ENERGETIC __________________ (slow, hard-working, active)
c NIMBLE __________________ (clumsy, good, happy, clever)
d CLUMSY __________________ (awkward, careless, merry)
e FLIMSY __________________ (silk, hard-wearing, soft)
f DUBIOUS __________________ (willing, certain, careless)

EXERCISE 31

SAMES AND OPPOSITES

Learn these words and find their meanings from your dictionary.
CONFLICT HARMONY GENEROUS CONTEMPTIBLE
PRAISEWORTHY CULTIVATED OCCASIONALLY INDULGENT

1 What are the missing words in the following? Use the words above.

a The __________ parents had spoiled their child.
b We are glad to have peace instead of __________.
c Try to live in __________, agreeing with one another.
d He was a __________ man and gave much to the poor.
e To ill-treat a dog is a __________ action.

2 Write out the words opposite in meaning to the words at the top of the page

3 In the following list of words write S if they have the same or nearly the same meaning and D if their meaning is different.

a INDULGENT ________________ strict
b CONFLICT ________________ strife
c HARMONY ________________ discord
d GENEROUS ________________ mean
e CONTEMPTIBLE ____________ admirable
f PRAISEWORTHY ____________ contemptible
g CULTIVATED ______________ wild
h OCCASIONALLY ____________ sometimes

4 From the words in the brackets find a word which means nearly the same or nearly the opposite of the first word. Write it in your exercise book. Then write S after it, if it is the same, and O if it is opposite.

a INDULGENT ______________ (lazy, strict, happy, free)
b CONFLICT ________________ (war, freedom, choice, bond)
c HARMONY ________________ (agreement, surprise, change)
d GENEROUS ________________ (give, take, mean, happy)
e CONTEMPTIBLE ____________ (despised, happy, proud)
f PRAISEWORTHY ____________ (contemptible, mean, pleasant)

EXERCISE 32

SAMES AND OPPOSITES

Learn these words and find their meanings from your dictionary.
EXTRAVAGANT SUFFICIENT HESITATE PROTECTED
DEFENCELESS DISCORD DEFICIENCY PRESENTLY ARTIFICIAL

1 Choose the missing words in the following from the list above.

a Do not __________ if you know the right way.
b We must be __________ against enemies.
c It was a brutal action to attack the __________ woman.
d The __________ man wasted his wages.
e These roses are __________, they have paper petals.

2 Write words opposite in meaning to the words at the top of the page.

3 In the following list of words write S if they have the same or nearly the same meaning and D if their meaning is different.

a HESITATE ____________________ pause
b PROTECTED ____________________ defenceless
c DISCORD ____________________ harmony
d EXTRAVAGANT ____________________ wasteful
e DEFENCELESS____________________ protected
f SUFFICIENT ____________________enough
g DEFICIENCY ____________________ sufficient
h PRESENTLY ____________________ now

4 From the words in the brackets find a word which means nearly the same or nearly the opposite of the first word. Put S after it if it means the same and O if the opposite.

a HESITATE ____________________ (stumble, stop, pause, hurry)
b PROTECTED ____________________(cared-for, ill-treated, lost)
c DEFENCELESS ____________________(waiting, unarmed, neglected)
d DISCORD ____________________ (happiness, disagreement, change)
e EXTRAVAGANT ____________________ (careless, wasteful, clever, proud)
f SUFFICIENT ____________________(much, more, over, enough)

EXERCISE 33

SAMES AND OPPOSITES

Learn these words and find their meanings from your dictionary.
POPULAR PAUSED FRIVOLOUS AMBIGUOUS ORDINARY LIQUID EXCELLENT ANCIENT

1 Choose the missing words in the following from the list above.

a He was good-natured and so was very __________ with other people.
b She was very __________ and was always behaving in a silly manner.
c He wore his __________ clothes for school.
d She __________ and looked behind her.
e He poured out the __________ into a large jug.

2 Write words opposite in meaning to the words at the top of the page.

3 In the following list of words, write S if they have the same or nearly the same meaning and D if their meaning is different.

a POPULAR __________________ unpopular
b PAUSED __________________ continued
c FRIVOLOUS __________________ silly
d AMBIGUOUS __________________ doubtful
e ORDINARY __________________ unusual
f SOLID __________________ liquid
g EXCELLENT __________________ poor
h ANCIENT __________________ modern

4 From words in the brackets find a word which means nearly the same or nearly the opposite of the first word. Put S after it for same, or O for opposite.

a POPULAR __________________ (known, liked, happy)
b PAUSED __________________ (continued, took, attack)
c FRIVOLOUS __________________ (silly, leave, pleased)
d AMBIGUOUS __________________ (doubtful, wanted, gain)
e ORDINARY __________________ (unusual, firm)
f SOLID __________________ (liquid, wood, box)

EXERCISE 34

SAMES AND OPPOSITES

Learn these words and find their meanings from your dictionary.
MODERN MEAGRE ATTRACTIVE PRUDENT EXHAUSTED
ENTHUSIASTIC FAMINE DISAPPOINT FRAGMENT MULTITUDE

1 Choose the missing words in the following from the list above.

a She wore an __________dress of bright coloured silk.
b When they reached the top of the hill they were __________.
c They lived in a very __________ way for they were very poor.
d When the __________ came many people died of starvation.
e He broke off a __________ of rock and threw it into the sea.

2 Write words opposite in meaning to the words at the top of the page.

3 In the following list of words write S if they have the same or nearly the same meaning and D if their meaning is different.

a MODERN ____________________ ancient
b MEAGRE ____________________ poor
c ATTRACTIVE ________________ pleasing
d PRUDENT____________________careful
e EXHAUSTED _________________ fresh
f ENTHUSIASTIC ______________interested
g FAMINE ____________________ plenty
h DISAPPOINT ________________ please

4 From the words in the brackets find a word which means nearly the same or nearly the opposite of the first word. Write the word in your exercise book. Put S after it for same, or O for opposite.

a MODERN ____________________ (some, never, ancient, one, again)
b ATTRACTIVE ________________ (ugly, plain, grim, grand)
c PRUDENT ___________________ (wise, idle, lazy, poor)
d EXHAUSTED _________________(fresh, bright, old, lame)
e ENTHUSIASTIC ______________(happy, interested, careless)
f FAMINE ____________________ (poor, old, lost, plenty)
g DISAPPOINT ________________ (try, lost, agree, please)

EXERCISE 35

SAMES AND OPPOSITES

From each of the following lists, write out the two which are alike but different from the others. The first is done for you.

1 metre, litre, gram, penny, kilogram (gram, kilogram)

2 John, Alice, Doris, William, Betty

3 penny, bag, cash, pound, purse

4 Winter, June, Friday, Summer, Christmas

5 Vicar, Mayor, King, Bishop, Doctor

6 General, Solicitor, Major, Prince, Mayor

7 hair, teeth, mouth, beard, head

8 church, house, chapel, shop, school

9 44, 50, 77, 20, 30

10 50, 19, 60, 28, 42

Write out the two words which are opposite in meaning in each of the following lists of words. The first is done for you.

11 giant, fairy, dwarf, tall (giant, dwarf)

12 closed, inside, open, deep

13 few, crowd, many, some, several

14 happy, pleasant, sad, beautiful

15 ancient, huge, modern, great, fine

16 melancholy, sorry, happy, worried

17 little, less, large, least

18 blunt, knife, sharp, clever

19 thrift, wise, waste, lost

EXERCISE 36

RHYMING WORDS

As I was sailing down the stream,
From far away, I heard a scream.

You will see at once that the words *stream* and *scream* have the same endings, and that these endings also have the same sound. We say that they rhyme; so that *stream* and *scream* are rhyming words.

I'd like to buy some honey.
But alas! I have no money.

In the two lines above, you see that *honey* and *money* have the same ending. Their endings also have the same sound. We say that they rhyme. *Honey* and *money* are rhyming words.

From these two examples we find that words ending with the same letters sometimes end with the same sound

Here is a short list of rhyming words. Read them aloud and notice that they end with the same letters, and that the sound of these endings is the same.

might __________	right	house __________	mouse
shade __________	trade	size __________	prize
stream __________	cream	length __________	strength
tame __________	same	tower __________	power
fate __________	rate	table __________	fable
flower __________	tower	blister __________	sister

Now from each of the following examples, write out the two (or more) rhyming words.

1 going, herring, string, strong, bring
2 mail, heel, coal, feel
3 frame, farm, came, firm
4 trade, cake, made, spade
5 sailor, beggar, doctor, tailor
6 troop, crop, droop, grope
7 earns, firms, barns, darns, dawns
8 page, edge, stage, badge
9 shade, catch, trade, watch

EXERCISE 37

RHYMING WORDS

Up against the window pane,
Pitter, patter, came the rain.

Read these lines aloud and you will see that the endings of pane and rain have the same sound. We say that *pane* and *rain* are rhyming words. You will have noticed that in this case, although the endings sound alike, they are spelt quite differently. Here is another:-

Overhead the swallows flew,
High into the skies so blue.

The rhyming words here are *flew* and *blue*, and again you will notice endings which sound alike, but the spelling is different: so now we know that rhyming words which sound alike may often be spelt differently.

Here is a short list of rhyming words. Read them aloud and notice that they rhyme, but are spelt differently.

lane	__________	pain	dough	__________	foe
bought	__________	taught	caught	__________	sort
cow	__________	bough	right	__________	bite
cuff	__________	rough	though	__________	so
bird	__________	curd	haste	__________	waist
haul	__________	tall	court	__________	port
heard	__________	purred	pair	__________	dare

Now from the following write the rhyming words:

1 meal, mail, feel, coal
2 rough, cuff, though, cow
3 blue, flew, flow, flee
4 freeze, freed, trees, agree
5 dough, rough, bowl, so
6 team, tame, seem, farm
7 comb, cough, dome, though
8 tower, mower, sour, sweet
9 pant, court, want, port
10 catch, kind, watch, find

EXERCISE 38

PROVERBS

1 Which two of these proverbs have almost the same meaning?

- **a** A STITCH IN TIME SAVES NINE.
- **b** EVERY LITTLE HELPS.
- **c** PREVENTION IS BETTER THAN CURE.

2 Pick out the two which mean almost the same in the following:-

- **a** THERE'S MANY A SLIP 'TWIXT CUP AND LIP.
- **b** NEVER COUNT YOUR CHICKENS UNTIL THEY ARE HATCHED.
- **c** PRIDE GOES BEFORE A FALL.

3 Two of these have almost the same meaning while one is different. Which one is different?

- **a** MANY HANDS MAKE LIGHT WORK.
- **b** LOOK BEFORE YOU LEAP.
- **c** TWO HANDS ARE BETTER THAN ONE.

4 Two of the following seem to contradict each other. Which?

- **a** MANY HANDS MAKE LIGHT WORK.
- **b** HE WHO HESITATES IS LOST.
- **c** TOO MANY COOKS SPOIL THE BROTH.

5 Which of the following statements has the same or nearly the same meaning as this proverb?

IT'S NEVER TOO LATE TO MEND.

- **a** Always do your darning late at night.
- **b** Never mend anything until it is completely worn out.
- **c** It is never too late to make a fresh start.

EXERCISE 39

PROVERBS

1 Which two of these proverbs have almost the same meaning?

a IT'S A LONG LANE WITH NEVER A TURNING.
b EVERY CLOUD HAS A SILVER LINING.
c MORE HASTE LESS SPEED.

2 Pick out the two which mean almost the same from the following:-

a DISTANCE LENDS ENCHANTMENT TO THE VIEW.
b THOSE WHO LIVE IN GLASS HOUSES SHOULD NOT THROW STONES.
c ABSENCE MAKES THE HEART GROW FONDER.

3 Two of these have almost the same meaning while one is different. Which one is different?

a MISFORTUNES NEVER COME SINGLY.
b MAKE HAY WHILE THE SUN SHINES.
c IT NEVER RAINS BUT IT POURS.

4 Two of the following proverbs seem to contradict each other. Which are they?

a HE WHO HESITATES IS LOST.
b FAINT HEART NEVER WON FAIR LADY.
c LOOK BEFORE YOU LEAP.

5 Which statement has the same meaning as this proverb?

EVERY CLOUD HAS A SILVER LINING.

a We get silver from the sky.
b Half a cloud is silver.
c There is a bright side to everything if we will trouble to look for it.

EXERCISE 40

WORDS IN ALPHABETICAL ORDER

Example 1
Arrange the letters in the word C U P B O A R D in correct alphabetical order.

Method
Write the letters in the given word exactly above the same letters in the alphabet.

A B C D O P R U
A B C D E F G H I J K L M N O P Q R S T U V W X Y Z

You will see at once that correct order is now A B C D O P R U. When you have tried several words in this way, you will find that you no longer need to write the letters above the alphabet, but can write them straight away.

Now place the letters of the following in correct alphabetical order:-

1 TABLE
2 CINEMA
3 METHODICAL
4 CERTAINLY
5 PROMISED

Example 2
Arrange the words LAW, LAD, LAY, LAG, LAP in correct alphabetical order, in the order in which they appear in your dictionary. You will see at once that all these words begin with LA.

Now look at the third letter of each word. These read:- W, D, Y, G, P. Arrange these 5 letters alphabetically and you will get:- D, G, P, W, Y. The correct order of the given words is therefore:- LAD, LAG, LAP, LAW, LAY.

Arrange the following words alphabetically. The first is done for you.

6 cap, cad, cat, cab, can — cab, cad, can, cap, cat
7 raw, ran, rag, rat, ram, ray
8 fag, fat, far, fad, fan
9 mat, mar, may, man, mad, map
10 pep, pew, pet, peg, pen
11 bag, bat, bay, ban, bar, bad
12 din, dip, dim, dig, did

EXERCISE 41

WORDS IN ALPHABETICAL ORDER

A B C D E F G H I J K L M N O P Q R S T U V W X Y Z

Example 1
Arrange the words BEE, BETTER, BEECH, BEN, BEER in alphabetical order.

You will see that all the words begin with BE, and the correct order is:- bee, beech, beer, Ben, better.

Arrange the following in correct alphabetical order.

1 pea, pear, pen, petal, peach

2 call, catch, card, cap, carp

3 dared, damp, dairy, danger, dark

4 scamp, school, scale, score, scared

5 tramp, trail, trap, trade, train

6 tool, tank, taken, tail, tame

7 feed, fate, food, fire, foot

8 look, lady, lock, lake, lane, lamp

9 made, mood, make, maid, more, mail

10 post, paint, penny, past, paid, pair

11 west, rest, most, want, caught

12 change, chance, charm, chalk

13 first, finish, flow, danger, dance

14 about, above, after, below, beneath

15 again, among, alone, around, abide

16 convict, keeper, cool, dawn, caught

17 middle, much, more, maid, make

18 Monday, Tuesday, Wednesday, Thursday, Friday, Saturday, Sunday

19 sweets, stew, plums, prunes, salad

20 games, football, guess, guide, found

EXERCISE 42

JUMBLED SENTENCES

The words in these sentences have been mixed up. Arrange them in their correct order. The first has been done for you.

1 four are seasons there *Answer :-* There are four seasons.

2 bakes the bread baker

3 works the fields the farmer in

4 in grow gardens flowers

5 green leaves are

6 uniform a soldier a wears

7 letters a delivers postman

8 football in team I play the

9 lessons have school in we

10 sweets like children

11 nests build birds

12 barks dog a

13 cooks mother my dinner the

14 with play I ball a

15 draw we pencil a with

16 sew cotton we with needle and

17 wood are chairs of sometimes made

18 books read we

19 songs the two sang choir

20 I bicycle ride a

21 my sharpened I pencil

22 have penknife I a

23 grass the cut the gardener

24 coat bought a new I

25 shoes bought I new

26 broken my is umbrella

EXERCISE 43

STATEMENTS

Example 1

CHILDREN SHOULD GO TO SCHOOL IF THEY WISH TO LEARN. *T.*

This statement is true and so we put the letter *T* after it.

ALL MEN ARE GIANTS. *F.*

This statement is not true for a giant is a very big person.
We therefore put the letter *F* after it for false.

Find out which of these statements are true and which are false, and write *T* or *F* in your exercise book.

1 We should go to school to learn.

2 Dwarfs are very tall.

3 Eggs grow on trees.

4 Apples are found in the ground.

5 A metre is longer than a kilometre.

6 A good shepherd looks after his sheep.

7 Children like sweets.

8 We should try to get to school early.

9 Growing children need plenty of sleep.

10 Hens lay eggs.

11 Lazy children work hard.

12 We wash with soap and water.

13 A dentist looks after our teeth.

14 We should brush our teeth with a tooth brush.

15 Computers are machines.

16 Some children like to watch television.

17 I am older than my teacher.

18 Flowers are beautiful.

19 Some pictures have frames.

20 A table is often made of wood.

EXERCISE 44

STATEMENTS

Read these sentences very carefully. Think what each one means. If the statement is true write *T* in your exercise book, and if false, write *F*.

1 A shower of rain lasts for hours.

2 A miner works in a coal mine.

3 Parents should look after their children.

4 Some animals are good for food.

5 Grass is the best food for people.

6 A knuckle is the name of a toe joint.

7 Breakfast is the first meal of the day.

8 All children wear green hats.

9 It rains every day.

10 Sunday is always a warm day.

11 All books have red backs.

12 Some pencils have points.

13 Children are never late for school.

14 A mouse is a very large animal.

15 We need a drink when we are thirsty.

16 We wash clothes to make them clean.

17 There are twenty-four hours in a day.

18 There are fifty pence in a pound.

19 A lion is a timid animal.

20 Houses are often made of bricks.

21 Fish always fly in the air.

22 Daffodils are always blue.

23 A buttercup is yellow.

24 Most people wear clothes.

25 We hear with our ears.

26 Beef comes from sheep.

27 There are twelve months in a year.

EXERCISE 45

STATEMENTS

The words in these sentences have been mixed up. Read them carefully and find out how they should have been written. Then write the correct sentence in your exercise book. If the correct sentence is true, write *T* after it, but if it is false write *F*.
The first two are done for you.

1 hives in live bees *Answer:* Bees live in hives *T*

2 circle a has sides four *Answer:* A circle has four sides *F*

3 milk us the gives cow

4 season the warmest is summer

5 boys hair all have dark

6 see a cannot dog

7 lot a people have of money poor

8 white is snow

9 girls hard work good

10 are printed books

11 have frames sometimes pictures

12 very diamonds precious are

13 badly good sing always singers

14 curly children all hair have

15 blue some eyes have people

16 cutting are scissors used for

17 rope is stronger cotton than

18 than winter summer warmer is

19 are in seasons four there year the

20 sometimes have meat we dinner for

21 die folk all young

22 sleep in kennel some a dogs

23 pencil a with we draw

24 sty lives in a pig a

25 boys hard lazy work

EXERCISE 46

STATEMENTS

In these jumbled sentences, there is one word which should not be there. It prevents the other words from making sense. Write this unwanted or extra word in your writing book, then with the remaining words write the correct sentence. If it is true, write *T* after it, and if it is false, write *F*.
The first is done for you.

1 wear all people Saturday glasses Here *Saturday* is the extra word.
The sentence should read:- All people wear glasses *F*

2 kind is a fuel sky of wood

3 summer beyond we in warm clothes wear

4 good always are earth people

5 day it rains yellow every

6 a make hundred pound one before pence

7 from made bread is holiday flour

8 false babies grass with teeth born are

9 food need children tame all

10 like sweets medicine children

11 always sun the is mountain cold

12 fruit an is apple a besides

13 all tomorrow children alike are

14 fine always is it weather

15 boat water a floats on walking

16 hard boy prize lazy a works

17 metal tomorrow lead is a

18 vegetable a cabbage nuisance is

19 is precious gold gallop

20 is sometimes chalk shoes white

EXERCISE 47

STATEMENTS

In these jumbled sentences, there is one word which should not be there. It prevents the other words from making sense. Write this unwanted or extra word in your writing book, then with the remaining words write the correct sentence. If it is true, write *T* after it, and if it is false, write *F*.
The first is done for you.

1 interesting a sometimes chair sit we on *Answer:* interesting. Sometimes we sit on a chair *T*

2 lay hens flowers sometimes eggs

3 puppy called is a beyond young a dog

4 false men have teeth fields all

5 round a train circle is

6 triangle three a cat has sides

7 to night bed we go sun at

8 a father than older son his chalk is

9 the by the time we pudding tell clock

10 a smaller than John hill mountain is a

11 leaves wanting trees have

12 in mirror ourselves bath a can see we

13 always clean tall if children are

14 is man a tall cabbage giant a

15 brother every has a garden girl

16 his gives away letter-box money a miser

17 fails who a full girl country marks receives

18 birthday last three times year silly came her

19 always lemons agree are sweet

20 from sheep purpose a wool comes

21 us cow animal the milk gives

22 water kettle in a boil newspaper we

23 boots made matches of leather some are

24 clothes makes washing clean house

25 blue tomatoes Saturday are

26 drink of cats milk

EXERCISE 48

STATEMENTS

In these jumbled sentences, there is one word which should not be there. It prevents the other words from making sense. Write this unwanted or extra word in your writing book, then with the remaining words write the correct sentence. If it is true, write *T* after it, and if it is false, write *F*.
The first is done for you.

1 die holiday never flowers *Answer*: holiday. Flowers never die *F*
2 get promise day every older we
3 love book parents children most their
4 sugar birthday sweet is
5 hero a Saturday coward is a
6 centimetres make until metre a one hundred
7 always yellow then is butter
8 camel until tree a in lives a
9 likes milk summer cat a
10 clothes morning we wear
11 Queen country surprise the rules the
12 paper is red precious not
13 wet flowers is water
14 carpet future a we walk can on
15 interesting depart are books some
16 grass lesson is brown always
17 knit pen we wool with
18 spring climb trees elephants
19 than faster aeroplanes were trains are
20 horses by hay eat
21 sing birds were sweetly
22 books games many play children
23 luggage never people spend holiday money
24 morning runs car lines on a
25 born we without are yesterday teeth

EXERCISE 49

COMPARISONS

Learn these words, and find what relationship they would have to yourself.

FATHER
MOTHER
SISTER
BROTHER
FATHER-IN-LAW
SISTER-IN-LAW
MOTHER-IN-LAW

COUSIN
NIECE
NEPHEW
GRANDSON

GRANDFATHER
GRANDMOTHER
GREAT GRANDFATHER
GREAT GRANDMOTHER
GRAND-DAUGHTER
BROTHER-IN-LAW

What are the missing words in the examples below? Choose the correct word from the brackets. The first is done for you?

1 As son is to father so is daughter to _mother_ (sister,mother,aunt)
2 As father is to son so is mother to __________ (brother, aunt,daughter)
3 As niece is to aunt so is nephew to __________ (father, sister, uncle)
4 As step-father is to step-mother so is mother to ______(son,aunt,father)
5 As man is to boy so is woman to __________(child, girl, sister)
6 As husband is to wife so man is to__________ (child, woman, girl)
7 Man is to manly as woman is to __________ (girlish, womanly)
8 Father is to fatherhood as mother is to __________(sister,motherhood)
9 Girl is to boy as queen is to __________(son, king, duke)
10 Girl is to boy as aunt is __________(lad, uncle, brother)

Fruits:- BANANA GREENGAGE POMEGRANATE PINEAPPLE STRAWBERRY PEACH.

The fruits of the Hawthorn tree are called HAWS.
The fruits of the Rose are called HIPS.

Vegetables:- CABBAGE CAULIFLOWER POTATOES CARROTS PARSNIPS TURNIPS.

What are the missing words in the comparisons below? You will find all the words you need in the brackets.

11 Pea is to pod as sword is to __________ (war, rifle, scabbard)
12 Cherry is to fruit as cabbage is to __________ (dinner, vegetable, dish)
13 Stem is to flower as flagpole is to __________ (country, flag, woods)
14 Apple is to apple-tree as grape is to __________ (tree, shrub, vine)

EXERCISE 50

COMPARISONS

Learn these parts of the body and where they are to be found.

ELBOW	JOINT	THIGH
WRIST	SHOULDER	ANKLE
CALF	KNEE	NOSTRILS
TEETH	THROAT	EYE-LID
FOREHEAD	WAIST	EYE-LASH.

Pick out the correct word in the comparisons below. You will find all the words you need in the brackets.

1 Lid is to eye as blind is to ____________ (table, window, ball)

2 Nostrils are to man as ________________ are to fish. (scales, gills, fins)

3 Leg is to knee as arm is to ____________ (hand, waist, elbow, sleeve)

4 Foot is to ankle as hand is to __________ (finger, nail, wrist)

5 Knee is to ankle as elbow is to _________ (arm, leg, wrist)

6 Head is to body as leaf is to____________ (branch, fruit, tree)

7 Ear is to hearing as eyes are to _________ (smell, taste, seeing)

8 Tongue is to taste as nose is to _________ (stone, tooth, smell, perfume)

9 Skin is to body as enamel is to _________ (door, tooth, stone)

10 Taste is to sight as tongue is to _________ (ears, eyes, mouth)

A doctor attends to the sick
A grocer sells groceries.
A plumber mends pipes.
A cyclist rides a bicycle.
A pianist plays the piano.
A minister preaches.

Now pick out the correct missing words in the examples below.

11 As bread it to food so is water to ________ (liquid, milk, drink)

12 As meat is to butcher so is bread to _____ (child, baker, flour)

13 As minister is to church so is teacher to ___(child, school, books)

14 As bicycle is to cyclist so is car to ______ (train, motorist)

15 As doctor is to hospital so is baker to _____(oven, bakery, shop)

16 As plumber is to pipes so is cobbler to ____(leather, shoes, last)

EXERCISE 51

COMPARISONS

Learn the following:-

A young hare is called a LEVERET.
A young swan is called a CYGNET.
A young bird is called a FLEDGLING.
A young fox is called a CUB.
A brood of small animals is called a LITTER.
A collection of books is called a LIBRARY.
A flock of birds is called a FLIGHT.
A large number of fish is called a SHOAL.
A collection of armour, or the place where it is kept, is called an ARMOURY.

Pick out the word which has been missed out in the following comparisons. You will find the words you need in the brackets.

1 As young is to old so is baby to________________ (child, boy, adult)

2 As cat is to dog so is kitten to ________________ (fur, mouse, puppy)

3 As wool is to sheep so is fur to ________________(cat, elephant, skin)

4 As wolf is to cub so is hare to ________________ (tail, leveret, burrow)

5 As feathers are to bird so is hair to ______________(skin, dog, tresses)

6 Sheep are to flock as bees are to________________(honey, swarm, hive)

7 Dog is to animal as robin is to ________________ (animal, insect, bird)

8 Sparrow is to bird as herring is to ________________ (insect, fish, sea)

9 Insect is to beetle as animal is to __________________(web, cow, fur)

10 Lion is to animal as ant is to __________________(bird, insect, world)

11 As cloth is to tailor so is leather to __________ (shoes, tools, cobbler)

12 As ship is to water so is aeroplane to _________ (land, air, passenger)

EXERCISE 52

COMPARISONS

Pick out the missing words in the following. You will find the word you require in the brackets.

1 Cattle is to herd as fish is to ______________ (catch, shoal, herring)

2 Pack is to wolves as ______________ is to birds. (sky, flight, cubs)

3 Birds are to migration as people are to ________(America, emigration)

4 Hoot is to the owl as bleat is to the ____________(wool, wise, sheep)

5 As soldier is to army so is ____________ to navy. (ship, sailor, sea)

6 As boat is to crew so is train to ______________(guard, passengers)

7 As neck is to necklace so is wrist to _________(beads, bracelet, hand)

8 As gloves are to hands so are shoes to _________(leather, feet, boots)

9 As hat is to head so is sock to ______________(wool, stocking, foot)

10 As shoe-lace is to shoe so is hair-ribbon to ________ (blue, hair, bow)

11 As clothes are to body so is paper to __________ (write, parcel, read)

12 As collar is to neck so is belt to ____________(waist, leather, dress)

13 As rain is to umbrella so is sunshine to _____ (parasol, tent, summer)

14 As car is to road so is train to ______________(ground, rails, water)

15 As wool is to sheep so is silk to _________ (goat, silkworm, material)

16 As cricket ball is to bat so is tennis ball to _____ (net, racket, player)

17 Bicycle is to one as______________is to two. (couple, tandem, ride)

18 Singing is to speaking as poetry is to ______ (prose, reading, reciting)

19 Green is to colour as square is to ____________(round, sides, shape)

20 Engine is to train as horse is to ________________(stall,cart, drive)

21 Lamb is to gentle as lion is to ______________(animal, strong, fierce)

22 Food is to eat as water is to __________________ (pure, tap, drink)

23 Thirsty is to drink as hungry is to ____________(starve, food, want)

24 Congregation is to church as________ is to theatre. (audience, crowd)

25 Audience is to theatre as__________are to football match. (collectors, spectators, players)

26 Window is to glass as door is to _____________(handle, wood, paint)

EXERCISE 53

COMPARISONS

Knives and forks are called CUTLERY.
Cups, saucers, plates, etc. are called CROCKERY.
Tables, chairs, etc. are called FURNITURE.
A THERMOMETER is an instrument for measuring HEAT.
A BAROMETER is an instrument for measuring the pressure of the ATMOSPHERE.

Pick out the missing words. You will find them in the brackets.

1 Straight is to crooked as new is to__________ (old, modern, wasted)

2 Wallpaper is to wall as carpet is to __________(ceiling, chair, floor)

3 Far is to near as up is to __________ (above, below, down)

4 Fire is to smoke as water is to __________ (liquid, rain, wet, steam)

5 Snow is to white as coal is to __________ (pen, work, letter, black)

6 Clay is to crockery as steel is to __________ (knife, cutlery, sword)

7 Bed is to lie as chair is to__________ (sit, stand, wood)

8 Knife is to blade as pencil is to __________ (write, point, draw)

9 Monday is to Tuesday as Thursday is to____ (Sunday, Friday, Saturday)

10 Grass is to green as snow is to __________ (cold, white, freeze)

11 Hear is to telephone as see is to __________ (sight, telescope, view)

12 Thermometer is to heat as barometer is to _____ (ton, gram, pressure)

13 Chalk is to blackboard as pencil is to __________ (draw, write, paper)

14 Scales are to fish as fur is to __________ (coat, animal, skin)

15 Wall is to room as frame is to __________ (wood, picture, fence)

16 Hook is to eye as button is to __________ (button-hole, shoe, coat)

17 Front is to back as top is to __________ (side, peak, bottom)

18 Purse is to money as pillar-box is to __________ (postman, red, letters)

19 Water is to fish as air is to __________ (animals, birds, sky)

20 Open is to closed as empty is to __________ (shut, full, window)

EXERCISE 54

COMPARISONS

Pick out the missing words in the following comparisons:-

1 As centimetre is to metre so is penny to _______ (silver, pound, money)

2 As kilometre is to distance so is hour to ___________ (time, clock, day)

3 Penny is to money as gram is to _________________ (purse, ton, mass)

4 Length is to long as _________________ is to wide. (area, width, round)

5 Square is to four as triangle is to ________________ (size, three, round)

6 Eyes are to two as fingers are to ___________________ (skin, ten, hand)

7 Pound is to penny as metre is to ___________ (centimetre, length, five)

8 Second is to two as third is to ____________________ (four, three, next)

9 Long is to short as high is to ____________________ (above, over, low)

10 Deep is to shallow as rough is to _______ (well, velvet, water, smooth)

11 1 dozen is to twelve as a score is to _____________ (ten, some, twenty)

12 Penny is to pound as centimetre is to __________ (length, metre, coin)

13 Oar is to boat as sails are to ____________________ (sea, yacht, water)

14 Sunday is to Saturday as August is to ____________ (winter, July, May)

15 Ten pence is to pound as millimetre is to __________________ (money, centimetre, kilometre)

16 Castle is to hut as giant is to __________________ (little, small, dwarf)

17 Lion is to mouse as eagle is to _______________ (bird, animal, sparrow)

18 Jam is to jar as butter is to _____________________ (drink, dish, brown)

19 Inside is to outside as interior is to ________ (above, exterior, beyond)

20 Solo is to duet as one is to ______________________ (song, two, child)

21 Book is to library as ship is to ___________________ (sea, fleet, sailor)

22 Work is to play as toil is to __________________ (week, leisure, enjoy)

23 Stockings are to legs as _________ are to arms. (hands, sleeves, fingers)

24 Swimming is to swimming pool as gardening is to ___________ (garden, school, man)

25 Milk is to cow as pork is to _______________________ (meat, pig, cheese)

EXERCISE 55

REASONING
(example only)

Example 1
The teacher wanted a child to come each day to give out the books before school commenced. Tom said that he could come only on Monday. John said that he could come any day. Rachel said that she could come only on Monday or Friday. Ravi said that he could come any day except Tuesday and Thursday. Susan said she could come any day except Thursday. It was finally settled to the teacher's satisfaction, so that one child came each day. Which child came on:-
1 Monday **2** Tuesday **3** Wednesday **4** Thursday **5** Friday?

Method of Working
Make a list of children, and after each name write the days on which each can come.

Tom	Monday				
Susan	X Monday	Tuesday	X Wednesday		X Friday
Rachel	X Monday				Friday
John	X Monday	X Tuesday	X Wednesday	Thursday	X Friday
Ravi	X Monday		Wednesday		X Friday

Now as Tom can come only on Monday that settles Monday, so we will put a cross against all the Mondays except the one opposite Tom's name. Now Rachel can come only on Monday or Friday. Monday is now taken so she must come on Friday. Cross out all the Fridays except that after Rachel's name. Ravi can come on Monday, Wednesday or Friday, but as Monday and Friday are taken, he will have to come on Wednesday. Cross out all Wednesdays except the one belonging to Ravi. Susan has now only Tuesday left, so she must take it. Cross out the other Tuesdays. John is now left with Thursday, so he must come on that day.

You can now read the answer from the chart above.

1 Tom comes on a Monday. **2** Susan, Tuesday.
3 Ravi, Wednesday. **4** John, Thursday.
5 Rachel, Friday.

EXERCISE 56

REASONING

When working the following problems read them very carefully, then make a chart for each one. This will help you to understand better.

1 Five children, Sarah, Maria, Dick, Tom and Runa arrived at the canteen when dinner was finished. The teacher at last managed to find five dinners, but they were all different. There was fish, cheese, ham, salad or sausages. She left them with the children and told them to settle things themselves. Now Runa could not eat anything but fish. Sarah said she was so hungry that she would eat anything. Tom liked everything except sausages. Dick only liked fish or cheese. Maria didn't like either salad or sausages. After much discussion each child had what he or she liked best. What did each child eat?

Sarah	Fish	Ham	Cheese	Salad	Sausages
Maria	Fish	Ham	Cheese		
Dick	Fish		Cheese		
Tom	Fish	Ham	Cheese	Salad	
Runa	Fish				

Make a chart before working the following:-

2 At a Christmas party every child was allowed to choose a present from the Christmas tree. At the end there were five children left to choose presents from the five presents which were left on the tree. These were a transformer, a racing car, a pony-toy, a felt-tipped pen set and a board game. Now Mary was well-behaved and said that she did not mind which present she was given. Aslam refused to have anything but the racing car. John said he wanted either the felt-tipped pen set or the board game. Tom said that anything would do for him except the pony-toy or the felt-tipped pen set. Jill said she would like either the racing car or the felt-tipped pen set. In the end it was arranged happily. Which present did each receive?

EXERCISE 57

REASONING

1 Five scouts were going on a picnic to a place some kilometres away. Unfortunately, they missed the bus and so had to find other means of making the journey. At last they procured a motor-cycle, a horse, a skateboard, a bicycle, and a pair of roller skates. Now A was the only one who could ride a motor-cycle. B couldn't ride a bicycle. C said he must have the skateboard. D would take anything. E said the roller skates were all he could manage. At last things were settled and the scouts set off. Who had the Skates, the Bicycle, the Skateboard, the Motor-cycle, the Horse?

A					Motor-cycle
B	Skateboard	Skates	Horse		
C	Skateboard				
D	Skateboard	Skates	Horse	Bicycle	
E		Skates			

2 Mrs Wilson was making dresses for her five daughters. She had five pieces of material - velvet, satin, cotton, silk, wool. Gemma said she must have the velvet because she was the eldest. Mary said she wanted either the velvet or the satin. Clare said she would be pleased with any material. Dorothy said she wanted the velvet, the satin or the silk, and Jean said she would have anything except the wool. Finally things were arranged to please them all. Who had the velvet, the satin, the silk, the wool, the cotton?

EXERCISE 58

REASONING

1 To get to the staff room John had to go up a staircase of 21 steps, along a short passage, then down a staircase of 14 steps. How many more steps up than down did he take on the journey there and back?

2 Tom is stronger than Bob, and Bob is stronger than John. Who is the weakest?

3 John is twice as old as Mary, and half as old as James. Who is the youngest, John, Mary, James?

4 One year a bazaar was held on three days, February 27th, 28th, 29th. Which year was it? (1988, 1983, or 1987)

5 Tom had three sisters, two brothers and a mother and father. How many were there in the family? (six, eight or seven)

6 Asma had more marbles than John but fewer than Dick. Who had the most marbles?

7 Mrs Jones buys three apples at five pence each and sells them to Mrs Davies for six pence each. Now Mrs Davies buys three apples at three pence each and sells them to Mrs Jones at four pence each. Who gains the most on the transaction?

8 At a certain town the shops closed on Wednesdays at one o'clock. John arrived on a certain day and found all the shops closed. What day was it? (Wednesday, Sunday, I do not know).

9 To get to her friend's house Jane walked 7 kilometres up hill and 5 kilometres down hill. How many kilometres down hill did she walk on the journey there and back?

10 Two children were set to run round a square field in opposite directions. They had number cards pinned on them and the winner was to receive a prize. They met half way round and being tired, changed cards and went back the way they had come. Why was this a foolish thing to do?

EXERCISE 59

REASONING

Write out the missing times in the following:-

	School starts	Continues	Ends
1	9 a.m.	____	12 - 30 p.m.
2	1 - 30 p.m.	2 hours 30 min.	____
3	9 -30 a.m.	____	12 noon
4	____	2 hours 15 min.	12 - 30 p.m.

5 If today is Wednesday, what was the day before yesterday? (Friday, Monday, Saturday)

6 If tomorrow is Friday, what was the day before yesterday? (Friday, Tuesday, Sunday)

7 If the 3rd of March was a Tuesday, on which day did the last day of March fall?

8 Dorothy is Mary's sister. She is also Clare's sister. What relation is Mary to Clare?

9 I have some yellow flowers. Daffodils are yellow. Are my flowers daffodils? (yes, no, I do not know)

10 I lost six red marbles. Tom found six red marbles. Were the marbles Tom found the ones I had lost. (yes, no, I do not know)

11 Tom is taller than John but not so tall as Fred. Which boy is the tallest?

12 Clare has more money than Susan, and Susan has more money than Jane. Who has the least money?

EXERCISE 60

REASONING

Which is the correct answer to each of the following, a, b, c ?

1 WE BOIL WATER TO

a make it hot.
b make it pure.
c make steam.

2 WE WEAR A WRIST-WATCH BECAUSE

a we wish to know the time.
b we wish to look our best.
c you cannot carry a clock with you.

3 PEOPLE RIDE BICYCLES BECAUSE

a they cannot walk.
b they are lazy.
c they can travel more quickly than walking.

4 WE PLAY SPORTS BECAUSE

a we are not wanted indoors.
b we wish to grow strong and healthy.
c people see us playing.

5 WE LEARN TO SING

a in order to annoy others.
b in order to give the singing teacher work.
c to give pleasure, and to give us a useful hobby.

6 WE PAINT THE OUTSIDE DOORS OF HOUSES

a to use up paint.
b to give people work.
c to prevent the wood from rotting.

7 WE READ BOOKS

a to pass the time.
b to gain knowledge.
c because they are boring.

EXERCISE 61

REASONING

Which is the correct answer to the following, a, b, or c ?

1 WE GO TO SCHOOL BECAUSE

a teachers need children to teach.
b we would be in the way at home.
c we wish to learn.

2 WE HAVE OUR HAIR CUT BECAUSE

a our hair never grows.
b it keeps it neat and tidy.
c hair clips are expensive.

3 WE CARRY A HANDKERCHIEF BECAUSE

a it looks nice.
b it makes a good paint rag.
c you cannot keep clean without one.

4 WE GO TO BED AT NIGHT BECAUSE

a there is nowhere else to go.
b we are afraid of the dark.
c the body needs rest.

5 WE WEAR CLEAN CLOTHES BECAUSE

a washing powder is cheap.
b we want to look smart.
c dirty clothes are comfortable.

6 BIRDS FLY AWAY IN WINTER BECAUSE

a they have promised to visit friends.
b they cannot stand our climate in winter.
c they think that we don't want them .

7 THE TREES SHED LEAVES IN AUTUMN

a to prepare for winter.
b because they like to see them blowing about.
c because they have turned brown.

EXERCISE 62

REASONING

What are the missing times in the following?

	Football commenced	The Game lasted	The Game ended
1	2 - 30 p.m.	1 hour 30 min.	_____
2	3 - 15 p.m.	_____	4 - 45 p.m.
3	_____	1 hour 45 min.	5 p.m.

What are the missing times in the following?

	Train Departs	Takes for Journey	Arrives at Destination
4	9 a.m.	_____	11 - 35 a.m.
5	10 - 45 a.m.	45 minutes.	_____
6	_____	1 hour 20 min.	3 - 55 p.m.

7 Jasbir is older than James, but younger than William. Who is the eldest?

8 Tea is dearer than sugar but cheaper than butter. Which of the three is the cheapest?

9 Tom has one sister, four boy cousins, John, Michael, Stephen and Gareth, and a girl cousin Jenny. How many cousins altogether has Stephen? (one, two, I do not know)

10 In a garden there were more blue flowers than white ones, but fewer blue ones than purple ones. Of which colour were there the most?

11 Tom broke a window. Mrs Johnson's kitchen window was broken. Did Tom break it? (yes, no, I don't know)

12 Robert's cat was missing from his home for two days. The newspaper said that a cat had been found dead in a stream. Was the dead cat Robert's? (yes, no, I do not know)

EXERCISE 63

PICKING OUT "ODD" WORDS

Look at these words:- chair, settee, bed, bench.
Bed is different from the others for they are names of seats.

Now look at these words:- cap, helmet, uniform, hat.
Here the "odd" or different word is *uniform*.

Write the odd or different word from the following. The first is done for you.

1 apron, overall, shirt, brush, blouse *Answer*:- Brush

2 coat, hat, shoes, pyjamas, key

3 helmet, cap, hat, finger

4 shoes, boots, coat, slippers, sandals

5 dress, coat, hat, jersey, shirt, T-shirt, clothes

6 blouse, overcoat, jacket, shirt, T-shirt, clothes

7 jersey, sweatshirt, shorts, pullover

8 shirt, trousers, waistcoat, dress

9 dress, suit, frock, blouse, outfit

10 overall, apron, bib, dress

11 silver, paper, gold, copper, tin

12 fifty pence, one pound, twenty pence, gram

13 metre, kilometre, hour, centimetre, millimetre

14 seconds, days, penny, years, hours

15 five pence, money, ten pence, one pound

16 hour, time, fortnight, month, week

17 twenty pence, fifty pence, coin, ten pence

18 ton, gram, mass, kilogram, milligram

19 half, quarter, third, fifth, one

20 some, several, many, few, none

EXERCISE 64

PICKING OUT "ODD" WORDS

Look at these words:- eye, ear, hand, leg, finger.
Finger is different from the other words for we have ten fingers, while we have only two hands, legs, ears or eyes.

Now look at the words:- doctor, matron, nurse, patient, hospital.
The "odd" or different word here is *hospital* for it is the name of a building, while the other words are all names given to persons.

Pick out the "odd" or different word from the following. The first is done for you.

1 coal, coke, wood, stone, peat *Answer:-* stone

2 kettle, pan, knife, fork, apron

3 cup, saucer, plate, dish, crockery

4 jug, plate, jar, bowl, dish

5 fork, knife-box, spoon, knife

6 dish, bowl, saucer, jug, jar

7 plate, mug, saucer, dish, cupboard

8 coal, wood, peat, coke, fuel

9 legs, arms, head, trunk, skin

10 neck, waist, wrist, chest, ankle

11 tennis, cricket, football, rounders

12 admiral, private, sailor, captain

13 policeman, postman, clergyman, clerk

14 novel, essay, poem, pamphlet, film

15 paint, crayon, board, chalk, pencil

16 fountain-pen, book, chalk, pencil

17 chapter, page, words, book, lines

18 bundle, parcel, pile, row, packet

19 rope, string, cord, pencil, thread

20 road, gate, street, avenue, lane

EXERCISE 65

PICKING OUT "ODD" WORDS

Example 1

PLUM, DAMSON, PEACH, APRICOT, *RASPBERRY*

Here the different word is "raspberry". The other fruits are alike because they all have a stone in the centre.

Now write down the "odd" words in the following. The first is done for you.

1 plum, damson, peach, raspberry *Answer:* raspberry

2 banana, orange, lemon, pear, fruit

3 orange, lemon, melon, pomegranate, tomato

4 tent, umbrella, parasol, sunshade, bed

5 roof, window, house, door, walls

6 manor, cottage, palace, mansion, castle

7 lion, tiger, elephant, bear, mouse

8 orange, lemon, pear, apple, potato

9 monkey, squirrel, leopard, tiger, animal

10 donkey, horse, tiger, dog, goat

11 attire, clothing, overcoat, raiment, apparel

12 box, jug, case, bin, tray

13 bucket, bin, sack, grate, tub

14 pillar-box, bin, tub, plate

15 chest, box, table, suitcase

16 carrier, plate, bag, purse

17 sack, bag, work-basket, tray

18 sieve, cup, colander, strainer, riddle

19 ice, snow, sunshine, frost, cold

20 rain, hail, frost, ice, weather

EXERCISE 66

PICKING OUT "ODD" WORDS

FAMILY, KIN, *FRIENDS*, RELATIONS, RELATIVES

Here the different word is "friends" because all the other words are names of people belonging to one's own family.

Now write down the "different" word in the following.
The first is done for you.

1 family, kin, friends, relations, relatives *Answer:* friends

2 mother, kin, father, sister, brother

3 brother, son, father, uncle, girl

4 mother, daughter, cousin, sister, aunt

5 spinster, widow, lady, sister, boy

6 mustard, salt, pepper, condiment

7 cinnamon, curry, spices, nutmeg

8 salt, pepper, plate, mustard

9 piano, violin, platform, cello, trumpet

10 violin, fiddle, instrument, organ, piano

11 Chester, Liverpool, Manchester, Essex, Preston

12 Brighton, Plymouth, Paris, Swindon, Bristol

13 York, Lancashire, Birmingham, Leeds, Derby

14 Man, England, Wight, Anglesey

15 Mersey, Dee, Snowdon, Tyne, Thames

16 Lancashire, Liverpool, Yorkshire, Cheshire

17 France, Ireland, America, Belgium

18 Europe, Holland, France, Spain, Denmark

19 England, Holland, Denmark, London

20 Halifax, Kent, Bolton, London, Bury

EXERCISE 67

MEANINGS

Learn these words and their meanings:-

A stevedore is a man who works in the docks.

A collier works down a coal mine.

A plumber is a person who mends pipes.

A smith is a person who shoes horses, he works at the forge, he uses hammer and anvil.

A carpenter makes things from wood.

A sculptor carves things in stone and marble, he uses a chisel.

A stone-mason cuts things out of stone.

A philosopher is a person who thinks about the meaning of life.

A novelist is a person who writes novels or books.

An author is a person who writes stories.

A poet is one who writes poetry.

A poacher is one who steals game.

A miser is one who hoards money.

A spendthrift is one who wastes money.

A hero is a brave person.

A benefactor is one who gives a benefit to another.

A scapegoat is one who is made to bear the misdeeds of another.

A monologue is a speech by one person.

A dialogue is a conversation between two or more people.

A solo is a song performed by one person.

A duet is a song performed by two people.

Autobiography is writing the story of one's own life.

Biography is a life story written by another.

EXERCISE 68

SIMILES

Learn these simple comparisons:-

As quiet as a mouse.

As dead as a door nail.

As keen as mustard.

As black as night.

As straight as a die.

As gentle as a dove.

As true as steel.

As clear as crystal.

As cunning as a serpent.

As deaf as a post.

As innocent as a child.

As timid as a hare.

As heavy as lead.

As smooth as velvet.

As red as a beetroot.

As vast as the ocean.

As greedy as a pig.

As cross as two sticks.

As poor as a church mouse.

As sweet as honey.

As slow as a snail.

As merry as a lark.

As hungry as a hunter.

As dry as dust.

As safe as houses.

As white as snow.

As swift as an arrow.

As brave as a lion.

As sly as a fox.

As white as a sheet.

As sharp as a needle.

As wise as an owl.

As green as grass.

As pure as untrodden snow.

As light as air.

As bright as silver.

As changeable as the moon.

As mad as a hatter.

As numberless as the sands.

As stubborn as a mule.

As rich as a millionaire.

As sour as vinegar.

As proud as a peacock.

As sick as a dog.

As busy as a bee.

As happy as a sandboy.

ANSWERS

TO

POPULAR

INTELLIGENCE

Exercise 1 - Obeying Orders

10	A	**12**	sentence	**14**	this	**16**	10
11	Z	**13**	of	**15**	this	**17**	20

Exercise 2 - The Alphabet

1	26	**7**	Q	**13**	G	**19**	19
2	A	**8**	Q	**14**	W	**20**	5
3	Z	**9**	W	**15**	J	**21**	U
4	MN	**10**	QRS	**16**	WXY	**22**	R
5	K	**11**	HIJ	**17**	Y	**23**	A
6	YZ	**12**	GHIJK	**18**	AZ	**24**	H

Exercise 3 - The Alphabet

1	N	**5**	S	**9**	T	**13**	BANANA
2	X	**6**	B	**10**	B	**14**	R
3	P	**7**	K	**11**	Q	**15**	R
4	N	**8**	B	**12**	4	**16**	E
						17	T

Exercise 4 - The Alphabet

1	Y	**5**	S	**9**	HLRHP	**13**	D
2	W	**6**	TTRPH	**10**	N	**14**	F
3	X	**7**	R	**11**	H	**15**	M
4	U	**8**	BNN	**12**	J	**16**	I

Exercise 5 - The Alphabet

1	K	**4**	A	**7**	K	**10**	A
2	T	**5**	Y	**8**	F		
3	H	**6**	G	**9**	COI		

Exercise 6 - Words Written Backwards

1	ALPHABET	**6**	ETALOCOHC	**11**	tops
2	ASTRONAUT	**7**	YTISORENEG	**12**	nips
3	DO YOUR BEST	**8**	YADHTRIB	**13**	stab
4	PHOTOGRAPH	**9**	KWꟻИ	**14**	rats
5	NONSENSE	**10**	ꟻ⊥OX	**15**	part

Exercise 7 - Words Seen in a Mirror

1	F	**6**	MOTOR	**11**	SCHOOL
2	ERCKS	**7**	MACHINE	**12**	PIANO
3	SIT DOWN	**8**	CAMERA	**13**	KITE
4	TRAP	**9**	BICYCLE	**14**	FOOTBALL
5	BOX	**10**	CLOCK	**15**	DONKEY

Exercise 8 - Code Writing

1 care	**3** pare	**5** hint	**7** lace
2 rose	**4** spent	**6** sail	**8** clap

Exercise 9 - Code Writing

1 MORE SCHOOLS HERE
2 CHILDREN DO HOME LESSONS
3 LINDA IS A NAME
4 CHARLES CAN SING

Exercise 10 - Code Writing

1 DIG
2 BOY
3 CAKE
4 CAN YOU PLAY THE FLUTE?
5 INK IS BLACK
6 GO HOME NOW
7 TAKE THIS LETTER TO THE POST OFFICE, PLEASE
8 19 1 25 14 15 20 8 9 14 7
9 23 15 18 11 8 1 18 4
10 19 20 1 14 4 19 20 9 12 12
11 EAT YOUR FOOD
12 DO YOUR BEST

Exercise 11 - Number Series

1 16	**6** 51	**11** 2	**16** 6
2 11	**7** 36	**12** 1	**17** 0
3 18	**8** 32	**13** 4	**18** 7
4 21	**9** 17	**14** 0	**19** 8
5 27	**10** 30	**15** 15	**20** 100

Exercise 12 - Number Series

1 243	**6** 1296	**11** 3	**16** $\frac{1}{3}$
2 64	**7** 162	**12** 3	**17** $\frac{1}{5}$
3 256	**8** 96	**13** 1	**18** $\frac{1}{6}$
4 625	**9** 1250	**14** 16	**19** 1
5 10000	**10** 729	**15** 3	**20** 1

Exercise 13 - Number Series

1 10	**5** 28	**9** 17	**13** 6, 5
2 9	**6** 1	**10** 8	**14** 22, 24
3 12	**7** 4	**11** 15, 17	**15** 6, 8
4 16	**8** 7	**12** 12, 11	

Exercise 14 - Number Series

1	29	**5**	23	**9**	22	**13**	30 or 35
2	42	**6**	29	**10**	38	**14**	12
3	21	**7**	66	**11**	1	**15**	12
4	32	**8**	42	**12**	4	**16**	8

Exercise 15 - Number Series

1	30	**5**	46	**9**	30	**13**	24
2	46	**6**	26	**10**	42	**14**	19
3	38	**7**	19	**11**	17	**15**	15
4	15	**8**	29	**12**	21		

Exercise 16 - Number Series

1	14	**4**	13	**7**	7	**10**	11
2	15	**5**	9	**8**	10		
3	17	**6**	4	**9**	10		

Exercise 17 - Number Series

1	$\frac{1}{14}$	**3**	$\frac{1}{13}$	**5**	$\frac{1}{12}$	**7**	$1\frac{1}{4}$
2	$\frac{1}{11}$	**4**	$\frac{1}{15}$	**6**	2	**8**	$1\frac{1}{4}$
						9	2

Exercise 18 - Numbers

1	6	**4**	4	**7**	5	**10**	9
2	3 and 9	**5**	8	**8**	24		
3	1 and 2	**6**	7	**9**	19		

Exercise 19 - Numbers

1	8	**4**	4	**7**	4	**10**	5, 6
2	1, 2, 5, 3	**5**	6	**8**	none		
3	10, 9, 7	**6**	3, 1, 2	**9**	7		

Exercise 20 - Letter Series

1	GH, IJ	**8**	OQS VXZ	**15**	UU, WW
2	MO,PR	**9**	WW, YY	**16**	GHW, IJV
3	EF, FG	**10**	PPP, TTT	**17**	MN, PQ
4	MP, PS	**11**	PM, TQ	**18**	UVW, XYZ
5	JKL, MNO	**12**	KL, NO	**19**	HG, JI
6	EV, FU	**13**	EV, UF	**20**	LKJ, ONM
7	JJ, LL	**14**	VE, UF	**21**	ON
				22	AC

Exercise 21 - Letter Series

1 8
2 8
3 11
4 9
5 B + C + D
6 A + C + D
7 B + C
8 C + D
9 B + A
10 A + B + C
11 C + D + E
12 A + E or B + D or A + B + C
13 A + B + C + D + E
14 D + E + A or B + C + E or A + B + C + D
15 E
16 A
17 6
18 3
19 C
20 B

Exercise 22 - Missing Numbers

1 3 9 1 6 − 1 4 **7** 8 = 2 4 3 8

2 6 **8** 3 0 4 − 4 2 9 8 7 = 2 5 3 1 7

3 7 4 6 3 − 2 8 5 **9** = 4 6 0 4

4 9 1 6 3 7 − 2 7 4 7 **8** = 6 **4** 1 5 9

5 9 **1** 4 7 − 2 8 7 5 = 6 2 7 2

6 8 6 4 6 3 − 2 0 9 **7** 4 = 6 **5** 4 8 9

7 2 **3** 7 X 5 = 1 1 8 5

8 4 0 **7** X 3 = 1 2 2 1

9 5 **6** 3 X 7 = 3 9 4 1

10 6 3 **5** X 5 = 3 1 7 5

Exercise 23 - Missing Numbers

1 6 7 1 3 6 − 2 8 4 **1** 9 = 3 8 7 1 7

2 2 **8** 7 1 3 − 1 5 8 7 6 = 1 2 8 3 **7**

3 9 6 0 2 7 − 4 3 8 7 **9** = 5 2 1 4 8

4 8 0 6 7 1 − 2 9 3 4 **7** = 5 **1** 3 2 4

5 8 **3** 7 1 5 − 2 9 4 7 6 = 5 4 2 3 9

6 6 6 3 5 8 − 2 7 6 **3** 9 = 3 **8** 7 1 9

Exercise 23 - Missing Numbers (continued)

7
2 **9** 3 ×
6
1 7 5 8

8
4 0 **6** ×
3
1 2 1 8

9
3 **1** 6 ×
5
1 5 8 0

10
4 7 **3** ×
9
4 2 5 7

Exercise 24 - Missing Numbers

1
6 7 3 1 –
2 8 **9** 7
3 8 3 4

2
8 6 6 9 –
2 **4** 7 3
6 1 9 6

3
9 6 1 7 –
2 8 0 **9**
6 **8** 0 8

4
8 **3** 4 6 –
2 9 7 8
5 3 6 8

5
3 **7** 6 2 5 –
1 5 9 1 6
2 1 7 0 9

6
3 **9** 8 4 5 –
2 5 9 3 6
1 3 9 0 9

7
2 **6** 3 ×
5
1 3 1 5

8
3 **5** 6 ×
8
2 8 4 8

9
4 **6** 3 ×
6
2 7 7 8

10
5 **3** 2 ×
7
3 7 2 4

Exercise 25 - Missing Words

1	outset	**11**	pan	**21**	pale
2	forefather	**12**	bad	**22**	beech
3	postman	**13**	star	**23**	buoy
4	becalm	**14**	sixty	**24**	grate
5	outside	**15**	seventy	**25**	would
6	underfed	**16**	third	**26**	bow
7	afterglow	**17**	second	**27**	waist
8	overhead	**18**	seventeen	**28**	pane
9	downcast	**19**	stun	**29**	sew
10	weatherbound	**20**	live	**30**	soar

Exercise 26 - Words and Numbers in Correct Order

2 Monday, Tuesday, Thursday, Friday, Saturday
3 two pence, five pence, ten pence, one pound
4 March, May, June, August, December
5 dawn, morning, noon, evening, night
6 seed, shoot, leaf, flower, fruit
7 1432, 1784, 1923, 1952
8 2354, 4536, 4567, 8765
9 minute, hour, week, fortnight, month
10 milligram, gram, kilogram
11 millimetre, centimetre, metre, kilometre
12 iv, v, vi, ix,x
13 2.7, 3.7, 4.6, 5.3, 9.1
14 5 a.m., 7 a.m., 2 p.m., 3 p.m., 4 p.m., 6 p.m.
15 eighth, quarter, half, one
16 6.15 a.m., 1.30 p.m., 2.30 p.m., 2.45 p.m., 4 p.m.
17 wash, dress, breakfast, walk, school
18 word, line, page, chapter, book
19 ii, iii, iv, v, viii
20 stand, loiter, walk, run
21 millimetre, litre, kilolitre
22 £0·50p, £1·25, £1·35, £3·67
23 grain, mill, flour, bread
24 two pence, ten pence, fifty pence, one pound

Exercise 27 - Sames and Opposites

1	**a**	conspicuous	**3**	**a**	S	**f**	D
	b	obscure		**b**	D	**g**	S
	c	expand		**c**	S	**h**	S
	d	transparent		**d**	S	**i**	D
	e	brief		**e**	D	**j**	D

2 opaque, transparent, obscure, conspicuous, expand, contract, pessimist, optimist, gradual, long

Exercise 27 - Sames and Opposites (continued)

4	a	clear	f	transparent
	b	visible	g	enlarge
	c	sudden	h	decrease
	d	short	i	optimist
	e	hidden	j	pessimist

Exercise 28 - Sames and Opposites

1	a	gradually	2	a	S		f	D
	b	monotonous		b	D		g	D
	d	perpetual		c	S		h	D
	d	magnify		d	S		j	S
	e	minimum		e	S		j	D

3	a	belittle	c	urge	e	slowly
	b	deter	d	magnify	f	highest

Exercise 29 - Sames and Opposites

1	a	fatigued	2	a	D	f	S
	b	rarely		b	D	g	S
	c	frequently		c	D	h	S
	d	superior		d	D	i	D
	e	abandon		e	S	j	D

3	a	exhausted	c	seldom	e	worse
	b	seldom	d	better	f	foolishness
					g	leave

Exercise 30 - Sames and Opposites

1	a	indolent	2	certain, dubious, energetic, indolent, clumsy, nimble, durable, learned, excess, moderation
	b	energetic		
	c	nimble		
	d	clumsy		
	e	flimsy		

3	a	S	d	S	g	D
	b	S	e	D	h	D
	c	D	f	S		

4	a	lazy	c	clumsy (O)	e	hard-wearing (O
	b	active	d	awkward	f	certain (O)

Exercise 31 - Sames and Opposites

1 a indulgent
b conflict
c harmony
d generous
e contemptible

2 harmony, conflict, mean, praiseworthy, contemptible, wild, frequently, strict

3 a D
b S
c D
d D
e D
f D
g D
h S

4 a strict (O)
b war (S)
c agreement (S)
d mean (O)
e despised (S)
f contemptible (O)

Exercise 32 - Sames and Opposites

1 a hesitate
b protected
c defenceless
d extravagant
e artificial

2 moderate, insufficient, decide, defenceless, protected, harmony, surplus, now, real or natural

3 a S
b D
c D
d S
e D
f S
g D
h D

4 a pause (S)
b cared-for (S)
c unarmed (S)
d disagreement (S)
e wasteful (S)
f enough (S)

Exercise 33 - Sames and Opposites

1 a popular
b frivolous
c ordinary
d paused
e liquid

2 unpopular, proceeded, serious, definite, extraordinary, solid, inferior, modern

3 a D
b D
c S
d S
e D
f D
g D
h D

4 a liked (S)
b continued (O)
c silly (S)
d doubtful (S)
e unusual (O)
f liquid (O)

Exercise 34 - Sames and Opposites

1 a attractive
b exhausted
c meagre
d famine
e fragment

2 ancient, plentiful, ugly, imprudent, fresh, disinterested, plenty, please, whole, few

Exercise 34 - Sames and Opposites (continued)

3	a D	c S	e D	g D
	b S	d S	f S	h D

4 a ancient (O) | b ugly (O) | c wise (S) | d fresh (O) | e interested (S) | f plenty (O) | g please (O)

Exercise 35 - Sames and Opposites

1 gram, kilogram
2 John, William
3 bag, purse
4 Winter, Summer
5 Vicar, Bishop
6 General, Major
7 hair, beard
8 Church, Chapel
9 44, 77
10 50, 60
11 giant, dwarf
12 closed, open
13 few, many
14 happy, sad
15 ancient, modern
16 melancholy, happy
17 little, large
18 blunt, sharp
19 thrift, waste

Exercise 36 - Rhyming Words

1 string, bring
2 heel, feel
3 frame, came
4 trade, spade or made
5 sailor, tailor
6 troop, droop
7 barns, darns
8 page, stage
9 shade, trade

Exercise 37 - Rhyming Words

1 meal, feel
2 rough, cuff
3 blue, flew
4 freeze, trees
5 dough, so
6 team, seem
7 comb, dome
8 tower, sour
9 court, port
10 kind, find

Exercise 38 - Proverbs

1 a and c
2 a and b
3 b
4 a and c
5 c

Exercise 39 - Proverbs

1 a and b
2 a and c
3 b
4 a and c
5 c

Exercise 40 - Words in Alphabetical Order

1 A B E L T
2 A C E I M N
3 A C D E H I L M O T
4 A C E I L N R T Y
5 D E I M O P R S
6 cab, cad, can, cap, cat
7 rag, ram, ran, rat, raw, ray
8 fad, fag, fan, far, fat
9 mad, man, map, mar, mat, may
10 peg, pen, pep, pet, pew
11 bad, bag, ban, bar, bat, bay
12 did, dig, dim, din, dip

Exercise 41 - Words in Alphabetical Order

1 pea, peach, pear, pen, petal
2 call, cap, card, carp, catch
3 dairy, damp, danger, dared, dark
4 scale, scamp, scared, school, score
5 trade, trail, train, tramp, trap
6 tail, taken, tame, tank, tool
7 fate, feed, fire, food, foot
8 lady, lake, lamp, lane, lock, look
9 made, maid, mail, make, mood, more
10 paid, paint, pair, past, penny, post
11 caught, most, rest, want, west
12 chalk, chance, charge, charm
13 dance, danger, finish, first, flow
14 about, above, after, below, beneath
15 abide, again, alone, among,around
16 caught, convict, cool, dawn, keeper
17 maid, make, middle, more, much
18 Friday, Monday, Saturday, Sunday, Thursday, Tuesday, Wednesday
19 plums, prunes, salad, stew, sweets
20 football, found, games, guess, guide

Exercise 42 - Jumbled Sentences

1 There are four seasons
2 The baker bakes bread
3 The farmer works in the fields
4 Flowers grow in gardens
5 Leaves are green
6 A soldier wears a uniform
7 A postman delivers letters
8 I play in the football team
9 We have lessons in school
10 Children like sweets
11 Birds build nests
12 A dog barks
13 My mother cooks the dinner
14 I play with a ball
15 We draw with a pencil
16 We sew with needle and cotton
17 Chairs are sometimes made of wood
18 We read books
19 The choir sang two songs
20 I ride a bicycle
21 I sharpened my pencil
22 I have a penknife

Exercise 42 - Jumbled Sentences (continued)

23 The gardener cut the grass
24 I bought a new coat
25 I bought new shoes
26 My umbrella is broken

Exercise 43 -Statements

1	T	5	F	9	T	13	T	17	F
2	F	6	T	10	T	14	T	18	T
3	F	7	T	11	F	15	T	19	T
4	F	8	T	12	T	16	T	20	T

Exercise 44 - Statements

1	F	7	T	13	F	19	F	25	T
2	T	8	F	14	F	20	T	26	F
3	T	9	F	15	T	21	F	27	T
4	T	10	F	16	T	22	F		
5	F	11	F	17	T	23	T		
6	F	12	T	18	F	24	T		

Exercise 45 - Statements

1 Bees live in hives *T*
2 A circle has four sides *F*
3 The cow gives us milk *T*
4 The warmest season is summer *T*
5 All boys have dark hair *F*
6 A dog cannot see *F*
7 Poor people have a lot of money *F*
8 Snow is white *T*
9 Good girls work hard *T*
10 Books are printed *T*
11 Pictures sometimes have frames *T*
12 Diamonds are very precious *T*
13 Good singers always sing badly *F*
14 All children have curly hair *F*
15 Some people have blue eyes *T*
16 Scissors are used for cutting *T*
17 Rope is stronger than cotton *T*
18 Summer is warmer than winter *T*
19 There are four seasons in the year *T*
20 Sometimes we have meat for dinner *T*
21 All folk die young *F*
22 Some dogs sleep in a kennel *T*
23 We draw with a pencil *T*
24 A pig lives in a sty *T*
25 Lazy boys work hard *F*

Exercise 46 - Statements

1	*Saturday*	All people wear glasses *F*
2	*sky*	Wood is a kind of fuel *T*
3	*beyond*	We wear warm clothes in summer *F*
4	*earth*	People are always good *F*
5	*yellow*	It rains every day *F*
6	*before*	A hundred pence make one pound *T*
7	*holiday*	Bread is made from flour *T*
8	*grass*	Babies are born with false teeth *F*
9	*tame*	All children need food *T*
10	*medicine*	Children like sweets *T*
11	*mountain*	The sun is always cold *F*
12	*besides*	An apple is a fruit *T*
13	*tomorrow*	Children are all alike *F*
14	*weather*	It is always fine *F*
15	*walking*	A boat floats on water *T*
16	*prize*	A lazy boy works hard *F*
17	*tomorrow*	Lead is a metal *T*
18	*nuisance*	Cabbage is a vegetable *T*
19	*gallop*	Gold is precious *T*
20	*shoes*	Chalk is sometimes white *T*

Exercise 47 - Statements

1	*interesting*	Sometimes we sit on a chair *T*
2	*flowers*	Hens sometimes lay eggs *T*
3	*beyond*	A young dog is called a puppy *T*
4	*fields*	All men have false teeth *F*
5	*train*	A circle is round *T*
6	*cat*	A triangle has three sides *T*
7	*sun*	We go to bed at night *T*
8	*chalk*	A father is older than his son *T*
9	*pudding*	We tell the time by the clock *T*
10	*John*	A hill is smaller than a mountain *T*
11	*wanting*	Trees have leaves *T*
12	*bath*	We can see ourselves in a mirror *T*
13	*if*	Tall children are always clean *F*
14	*cabbage*	A giant is a tall man *T*
15	*garden*	Every girl has a brother *F*
16	*letter-box*	A miser gives away his money *F*
17	*country*	A girl who fails receives full marks *F*
18	*silly*	Her birthday came three times last year *F*
19	*agree*	Lemons are always sweet *F*
20	*purpose*	Wool comes from a sheep *T*
21	*animal*	The cow gives us milk *T*
22	*newspaper*	We boil water in a kettle *T*
23	*matches*	Some boots are made of leather *T*
24	*house*	Washing makes clothes clean *T*
25	*Saturday*	Tomatoes are blue *F*
26	*of*	Cats drink milk *T*

Exercise 48 - Statements

1	*holiday*	Flowers never die *F*
2	*promise*	Every day we get older *T*
3	*book*	Most parents love their children *T*
4	*birthday*	Sugar is sweet *T*
5	*Saturday*	A hero is a coward *F*
6	*until*	A hundred centimetres make one metre *T*
7	*then*	Butter is always yellow *T*
8	*until*	A camel lives in a tree *F*
9	*summer*	A cat likes milk *T*
10	*morning*	We wear clothes *T*
11	*surprise*	The Queen rules the country *T*
12	*red*	Paper is not precious *T*
13	*flowers*	Water is wet *T*
14	*future*	We can walk on a carpet *T*
15	*depart*	Some books are interesting *T*
16	*lesson*	Grass is always brown *F*
17	*pen*	We knit with wool *T*
18	*spring*	Elephants climb trees *F*
19	*were*	Aeroplanes are faster than trains *T* or Trains are faster than aeroplanes *F*
20	*by*	Horses eat hay *T*
21	*were*	Birds sing sweetly *T*
22	*books*	Many children play games *T*
23	*luggage*	People never spend holiday money *F*
24	*morning*	A car runs on lines *F*
25	*yesterday*	We are born without teeth *T*

Exercise 49 - Comparisons

1	mother	5	girl	9	king	13	flag
2	daughter	6	woman	10	uncle	14	vine
3	uncle	7	womanly	11	scabbard		
4	father	8	motherhood	12	vegetable		

Exercise 50 - Comparisons

1	window	5	wrist	9	tooth	13	school
2	gills	6	tree	10	eyes	14	motorist
3	elbow	7	seeing	11	drink	15	bakery
4	wrist	8	smell	12	baker	16	shoes

Exercise 51- Comparisons

1	adult	4	leveret	7	bird	10	insect
2	puppy	5	dog	8	fish	11	cobbler
3	cat	6	swarm	9	cow	12	air

Exercise 52 - Comparisons

1	shoal	8	feet	15	silkworm	22	drink
2	flight	9	foot	16	racket	23	food
3	emigration	10	hair	17	tandem	24	audience
4	sheep	11	parcel	18	prose	25	spectators
5	sailor	12	waist	19	shape	26	wood
6	passengers	13	parasol	20	cart		
7	bracelet	14	rails	21	fierce		

Exercise 53 - Comparisons

1	old	6	cutlery	11	telescope	16	button-hole
2	floor	7	sit	12	pressure	17	bottom
3	down	8	point	13	paper	18	letters
4	steam	9	Friday	14	animal	19	birds
5	black	10	white	15	picture	20	full

Exercise 54 - Comparisons

1	pound	8	three	15	centimetre	22	leisure
2	time	9	low	16	dwarf	23	sleeves
3	mass	10	smooth	17	sparrow	24	garden
4	width	11	twenty	18	dish	25	pig
5	three	12	metre	19	exterior		
6	ten	13	yacht	20	two		
7	centimetre	14	July	21	fleet		

Exercise 56 - Reasoning

1 Sarah: sausages; Maria: Ham; Dick: Cheese; Tom: Salad; Runa: Fish.

2 Mary: Pony-toy; Aslam: Racing-car; John: Board game; Jill: Felt-tipped pens; Tom: Transformer

Exercise 57 - Reasoning

1 A – Motor-cycle; B – Horse; C – Skateboard; D – Bicycle; E – Skates.

2 Gemma: Velvet; Mary: Satin; Dorothy: Silk; Jean: Cotton; Clare: Wool.

Exercise 58 - Reasoning

1	Both the same	4	1988	7	Both the same
2	John	5	Eight	8	I do not know
3	Mary	6	Dick	9	12 kilometres
				10	Both ran the same distance

Exercise 59 - Reasoning

1	3 h. 30 min.	5	Monday	9	I don't know
2	4 p.m.	6	Tuesday	10	I don't know
3	2 h. 30 min.	7	Tuesday	11	Fred
4	10 - 15 a.m.	8	Sister	12	Jane

Exercise 60 - Reasoning

1	a	2	a	3	c	4	b
5	c	6	c	7	b		

Exercise 61 - Reasoning

1	c	2	b	3	c	4	c
5	b	6	b	7	a		

Exercise 62 - Reasoning

1	4 p.m.	2	1 h. 30 min.	3	3-15 p.m.
4	2 h. 35 min.	5	11-30 a.m.	6	2-35 p.m.
7	William	8	sugar	9	I don't know
10	purple	11	I don't know	12	I don't know

Exercise 63 - Picking out "Odd" words

1	brush	6	clothes	11	paper	16	time
2	key	7	shorts	12	gram	17	coin
3	finger	8	dress	13	hour	18	mass
4	coat	9	outfit	14	penny	19	one
5	clothes	10	dress	15	money	20	none

Exercise 64 - Picking out "Odd" words

1	stone	6	saucer	11	football	16	book
2	apron	7	cupboard	12	private	17	book
3	crockery	8	fuel	13	clerk	18	row
4	plate	9	skin	14	film	19	pencil
5	knife-box	10	chest	15	board	20	gate

Exercise 65 - Picking out "Odd" words

1	raspberry	6	cottage	11	overcoat	16	plate
2	fruit	7	mouse	12	tray	17	tray
3	tomato	8	potato	13	grate	18	cup
4	bed	9	animal	14	plate	19	sunshine
5	house	10	tiger	15	table	20	weather

Exercise 66 - Picking out "Odd" words

1	friends	6	condiment	11	Essex	16	Liverpool
2	kin	7	spices	12	Paris	17	America
3	girl	8	plate	13	Lancashire	18	Europe
4	cousin	9	platform	14	England	19	London
5	boy	10	instrument	15	Snowdon	20	Kent